Readymade CVs

FIFTH EDITION

Readymade CVs

LYNN WILLIAMS

KoganPage

LONDON PHILADELPHIA NEW DELHI

First published in Great Britain and the United States in 1996 by Kogan Page Limited
Second edition 2000
Third edition 2004
Fourth edition 2009
Fifth edition 2012

120 Pentonville Road
London N1 9JN
United Kingdom
www.koganpage.com

© Lynn Williams, 1996, 2000, 2004, 2009, 2012

The right of Lynn Williams to be identified as the author of this work has been asserted by her in accordance with the Copyright, Designs and Patents Act 1988.

The views expressed in this book are those of the author, and are not necessarily the same as those of Times Newspapers Ltd.

ISBN   978 0 7494 6505 6
E-ISBN   978 0 7494 6506 3

British Library Cataloguing-in- Publication Data

A CIP record for this book is available from the British Library

Typeset by Graphicraft Ltd, Hong Kong
Printed and bound in India by Replika Press Pvt Ltd

Contents

You always need a great CV

Even a few years ago, unless you were either very ambitious or very unlucky you could expect to go to work in an organisation straight from school or college and stay there, gradually moving up the promotion ladder until you retired. Today, career advancement is more uncertain. Most people will change jobs several times during their working lives; some will even change careers. Increasingly, a good CV is an essential tool in the survival kit of every employee.

What is a good CV, though? The short answer is: one that gets you an interview for the job you want.

Imagine you're the employer for a moment. You have 150 CVs on your desk and from them you have to choose just a handful of applicants to interview. What are you looking for? How do you decide? My bet is that you would pick people who look as though they know how to do the job. People, that is, who:

- have the skills the job requires;
- have experience relevant to the job;
- have successfully handled similar challenges in the past.

As an employer with 150 career histories to read, you would be grateful, too, to the people who made those facts easy to find on their CV.

This book is about making those facts easy to find, and how to highlight them to your best advantage. The first five chapters look in detail at what is in a CV – how to select what goes in and what stays out, layout and presentation, and how to make a good first impression.

Few people, however, have absolutely straightforward careers, and some CVs are trickier to write than others, so Chapters 6 to 9 look at some of the problems that people encounter, and how to handle them. They show how, by highlighting key parts of your CV, you can emphasise your strengths rather than stressing your weaknesses. They also look at CVs for specific 'tricky' situations – getting your first job, returning to work after a career break, and continuing in work as a mature employee or after retirement.

The remaining chapters give further examples of CVs. These are written especially for specific categories of jobs – creative positions, sales vacancies, managerial posts, and so on. Different types of job often emphasise different features when it comes to what makes a person right for that position. Some jobs rely heavily on personal qualities, some demand specific academic qualifications, while others require evidence of achievement in that particular field. These chapters show how, by highlighting and strengthening the relevant parts of your CV, you can emphasise these key points and put them across to a prospective employer effectively.

The final chapter gives you a host of action verbs, positive descriptions and desirable benefits so that you need never again be lost for words when writing your CV.

This book also shows you how to use two special sections of your CV to tailor it specifically for each and every job you apply for so that your suitability for the position stands out so well that an employer would need a really good reason *not* to interview you. Most of the example CVs you will see here have been customised in this way.

Whether you're looking for your first job, aiming for promotion or applying for the job of your dreams, you can put together a great CV that shows your future employer your skills and experience clearly and concisely – these examples show you how.

If you want to, you can follow the layout of the CV examples in this book to compile your own CV. Each, when printed on to A4 paper, runs to two pages – the recommended length for a CV. Each example puts the key facts and the high-priority information that tells an employer you know how to do the job on the front page, with back-up and lower-priority details on the second page.

To make things even easier for you, you can find downloadable templates for each of the job-specific CVs along with further useful examples of job-search letters at **www.koganpage.com/editions/readymade-CVs/9780749465056**. Use the resources on this site along with the information in this book to remove any trace of doubt or uncertainty you may have about writing your CV and covering letter, and ensure that your application stands out from the crowd.

Chapter One
The basic CV

The aim of your CV

Your CV is a summary of your career history, and the skills and experience you have gained during the course of it. So, when you send it off to an employer, you will naturally want it to:

- attract attention;
- create a good impression;
- present your relevant skills and qualities clearly and concisely.

The main purpose of your CV is to show that you have the necessary qualities and qualifications to do the job you're applying for. The aim is to get you an interview with that employer, so it needs to demonstrate clearly that you have:

- the specific skills needed for the job;
- the right sort of experience for the job;
- the personal qualities for the position;
- an understanding of the specific requirements of the job.

Getting your CV read

The first obstacle is to get your CV read. Vacancies often attract hundreds of replies, and even the most conscientious employers can't digest every CV that crosses their desk. The best way to make sure that yours is the one that gets noticed is to: keep it simple.

Keep it simple

The easier your CV is to read, the better, so:

- **Keep it short.** Two A4 pages are the perfect length for most people.
- **Keep it clear.** A CV should be well laid out with wide margins, clear section headings, and the information organised in a logical, easy-to-follow way.
- **Keep it relevant.** The employer has just one question in mind when looking at an employee or potential employee: Can this person do the job? Make sure your CV answers that question positively.

Creating an impression

As well as keeping your CV short, clear and relevant, make it look businesslike and professional too.

Use:

- good-quality, plain white or cream A4-size paper;
- a good, clear font, usually in black;
- short, clearly headed sections that display your key points at a glance;
- bullet points, capital letters and underlining discreetly to condense and emphasise information.

Avoid:

- spelling and grammar mistakes;
- alterations and amendments – print off a fresh, correct copy.

The following pages give a template for a two-page CV, showing what goes where, followed by an example of a completed CV.

(**Your Name** in large, bold type)
(Your full address)

_____

_____

_____

(Postcode)
(Telephone number, including area code)
(E-mail address)

Career profile

(A brief, businesslike description of yourself)

(Skills)

(Experience)

(Personal strengths)

Key strengths

(Your skills, experience and personal qualities that most closely match

the job requirements)

Key skills

- *(The main skills you have developed)*

- *(Particularly those appropriate to the job you are applying for)*

-

-

-

Career history

(**Name of company**, usually starting with the most recent)
(Dates you worked there)

(Job title)
(Brief description of what you did)
(Brief description of what you achieved in this position)

- _____

- _____

- _____

(Name of company)
(Dates you worked there)
(Job title)
(Brief description of what you did)
(Brief description of what you achieved in this position)

- _____

- _____

- _____

(Name of company)
(Dates you worked there)
(Job title)
(Brief description of what you did)
(Brief description of what you achieved in this position)

- _____

- _____

- _____

Education and training

(Start with the highest, most recent _or_ most relevant qualification)
(Name of school, college or university)

(Dates you attended)

(The qualification you achieved)

(You could include brief details of what was covered in the course, especially if recently qualified)

- _____

- _____

- _____

(Name of school, college or university)

(Dates you attended)

(The qualification you achieved)

(Name of school, college or university)

(Dates you attended)

(The qualification you achieved)

(Don't go back further than your senior or secondary school)

(Professional training)

(Details of any professional training undertaken at work)

- (Qualification or skill achieved)

-

-

-

-

Personal details

(Date of birth)

(Driving licence)

(Married or single – only if relevant)

(Nationality – only if relevant)

(Interests and activities. Brief details)

(References – usually 'available on request')

Robert Dalesman
2 Woodland Drive
Sandacre
West Lea
Norfolk NR4 5TE

Tel: 00000 000000
E-mail: rdalesman@anyisp.com

Career profile

A company representative with experience of both sales and distribution with a major company, and the proven ability to meet and surpass sales targets, now keen to move ahead in a challenging sales position with a market leader.

Key strengths

Organisation and initiative: personally responsible for reorganising sales route to reduce costs and maximise profit, increasing turnover by 55 per cent.

Sales, marketing or distribution experience: four years' practical knowledge of sales and distribution; currently completing two-year open-learning course covering all aspects of sales and marketing.

Drive and enthusiasm: turned an underperforming route into a highly profitable one. Gained new accounts and developed existing ones by establishing customer needs and preferences. Undertook Certificate in Sales and Marketing in own time and at own expense in order to further career.

Key skills

- Developing customer relationships from cold call to repeat order
- Recognising sales opportunities
- Identifying customer needs
- Organising daily and weekly schedules
- Managing customer credit control and discount negotiation
- Currently working towards Certificate in Sales and Marketing

Career history

Penbury Foods Ltd
2009 to present
Van Sales Representative
Delivered orders to current customers and developed new and existing accounts, including introduction of new lines and products.
  Turned a subsidised delivery route into a profit-making sales territory:

- Reorganised two sales routes into one, thereby reducing costs
- Increased turnover by 55% in first six months
- Increased overall turnover by £2,500 per week

Dann Farms Ltd
2007 to 2009
Customer Deliveries Organiser
Organised weekly schedule of perishable product deliveries to super-market outlets nationally. Supervised four-man delivery team, and liaised with Transport and Administration Department to coordinate delivery schedules.

Lockings Distribution
2002 to 2007
Van Driver
Part of the Lockings Distribution Fleet. Delivered food products to supermarket chains, in accordance with a strict timetable. Maintained daily record logs. Responsible for maintaining vehicle to company standards. Promoted within company from previous position as general loader and driver.

Education and training

Somerston College
2000 to 2002
City and Guilds Warehousing and Distribution

Lea Park School
1995 to 2000
Total of five GCSEs gained, including Maths and English

Professional training

Eastern Institute of Marketing
From September 2010

Certificate in Sales and Marketing
Two-year open-learning course covering all aspects of professional sales including:

- Principles of selling
  - pricing and profit
  - negotiation
  - sales promotions
  - sales opportunities
  - advanced selling techniques
  - managing client accounts
  - developing client business
- Managing sales territories
- Finance for sales and marketing
- Law for sales and marketing
- Forecasting and analysis

Personal details

Date of birth:	10 April 1984
Driving licence:	Full, clean UK
Interests:	A keen interest in sport and keeping fit, and play regularly for a local Sunday football team
References:	Available on request

Include

✓ **Your skills and experience, knowledge and capabilities.** Your relevant experience and competence are the most important things to put in your CV. Match them as closely as possible to those required by the job.

✓ **Skills and qualifications that feature in the job advertisement.** If you are responding to an advertised vacancy, or if you have a comprehensive job description, make use of it. This is covered more fully in Chapter 3.

✓ **Your achievements.** A CV is not the place for false modesty: achievements need to be spelled out clearly. Employers rarely have time to search out information, and should be able to see at a glance exactly what you can offer them.

✓ **Put the most important information on the first page.** If your CV runs to two pages, make sure the first page is the most interesting and highlights your key points.

Leave out

✕ **Unnecessary personal details.** You can safely leave out:

Marital status	Religious affiliation
Maiden name	Political affiliation
Number of children	Age (in addition to date of birth)
Ages of children	Previous salary
Nationality	Reason for leaving last job
Gender	Photographs
Partner's occupation	

✕ **Negative information.** While it's unwise to lie in your CV, you don't have to include information that will diminish your chance of an interview – as long as it doesn't affect your ability to do the job. Always put things in the most positive way that you can.

× **Out-of-date and irrelevant information.** Things that happened more than 10 years ago are of very little interest unless they have a direct bearing on your present capabilities. What you are doing currently is much more relevant.

× **References.** If references are required, they will be taken up later. There is no need to put the names and addresses of referees on your CV.

Finally

When you send your CV, remember the following:

- Always send your CV to a named individual within the company, not just to The Personnel Department. If you don't know the name of the person to send it to, ring up and find out.

- Include a covering letter written specifically to match the requirements of that job.

- The letter should be as well presented as your CV and typed on good-quality, white or cream, A4 paper.

- Send your CV and covering letter unfolded in a white or cream A4-size envelope. Don't try to save on postage by cramming it into a smaller envelope.

- If there is a closing date, make sure your application is sent off in good time. Applications received after the deadline are rarely, if ever, considered.

Any questions?

Should I put it in or leave it out?

There are two basic questions to ask yourself when considering whether or not to put an item of information into your CV:

- Will it encourage them to interview me?
- Will it discourage them from interviewing me?

If the answer to the first question is an emphatic yes, put it in. If, however, you feel less certain, think carefully about including it. Could the space be used more effectively to expand on something more important?

If you answer yes to the second question, leave it out.

Chapter Two
Your CV section by section

Information is easier to digest when it's sorted into small, clearly labelled portions. As you may have already noticed, each CV in this book is divided into clear, easy-to-read sections:

Career profile

Key strengths

Key skills

Career history

Education and training

Personal details

This chapter looks at each of these sections in more detail.

Section 1 – the career profile

This is a brief statement that summarises your background and experience. We'll look at this section in great detail in Chapter 3.

Section 2 – key strengths

We'll also look at this in detail in Chapter 3. It is, briefly, a section highlighting the most important skills, experience and personal qualities that make you the right person for the job.

These are the two sections you will customise so that each CV is tailor-made for the job you want.

Meanwhile, let's continue with the rest of your CV so that you have it organised and prepared ready for those final details to be added when you apply for a job.

Section 3 – your key skills

Including a section that highlights your key skills can save anyone reading your CV a lot of time and effort. So use this section to summarise and emphasise your key skills and abilities, qualifications or achievements.

Key skills

Example 1

- Keyboard skills – 40 wpm
- Operation of
  - fax machine
  - photocopiers – Canon and Rank Xerox
  - franking machine
- Preparing and writing routine correspondence
- Organising and carrying out routine administrative work
  - maintaining records
  - dealing with incoming telephone calls
  - dealing with incoming mail

Example 2

- Carrying out routine security procedures
- Monitoring security equipment including alarms and surveillance cameras
- Checking and verifying all incoming personnel including deliveries
- Carrying out routine checking and maintenance of safety equipment

Key qualifications

Example 1

- RSA III Typewriting – current speed 70 wpm
- RSA II Audio-typing – current speed 70 wpm
- RSA II Shorthand – current speed 120 wpm
- RSA Certificate in Computer Literacy and Information Technology:
    - Microsoft Office:
    - Word
    - Excel
    - Access

Example 2

- BSc Mechanical Engineering
- Practical experience of programming:
    - CNC machinery
    - CMM
    - Robots
- Use of CAD/CAM systems
- Computer programming languages:
    - C++
    - FORTRAN
    - COBOL

Key achievements

Example 1

- Developing key ranges, many of which reached top ten leading brand status, including:
    - freeze-dried pasta sauces
    - savoury snack rice
    - fresh chilled soups
- Improving processing methods in natural-set department, reducing spoilage and improving profit margins
- Reducing wastage in thick-set yoghurt department with similar effect
- Consistently bringing processing trials in to time and on budget

Example 2

- Successfully managing, training and motivating 20 staff in three branches, thereby exceeding targets for insurance, savings and mortgage lending sales

- Organising and opening two new suburban branch offices, and exceeding forecast transaction levels by 25% in the first year of operation

- Organising full relocation of group departments to new premises within strict deadlines

- Devising and delivering OLE and DDL training to Sales Support staff, enabling them to use data analysis tools; and to Secretarial staff, enabling them to produce presentations, graphs and organisation charts, and to maximise efficient system usage

- Designing and providing user-friendly computer spreadsheet for Commercial Lending Sales Team, enabling them to project lending terms and reduction of capital balances for given varying repayment possibilities

Section 4 – your career history

Your career history tells a prospective employer what you have done and where and when you have done it.

For each entry in your career history section, include:

- the name of the company, starting with the most recent;
- the dates you worked there;
- your job title or position;
- the main responsibilities of that position – a brief description of what you did;
- your key achievements during your time there.

Example 1

K&L Polton
2005 to 2011
Human Resources Manager

Trained, assessed and developed staff at all levels:

- Responsible for 750 employees
- Devised and introduced new appraisal system for all departments, based on performance assessment and linked to performance-related pay structure

- Trained in-house assessors for new system
- Initiated use of interactive software for staff development in areas other than IT training
- Supervised a professional training team of 10

Example 2

Axon Business Machines
2006 to 2012
Sales Executive
Appointed to direct sales role. Responsible for meeting targets on sales of office equipment in business-to-business environment.
Achievements include:

- Directed highly successful sales team to top company awards
- Increased profit margins by more than 10%
- Won Top Salesperson Award two years in succession
- Achieved more than 100% increase in technical support revenue budgets

Example 3

Safe As Houses
2009 to present
Volunteer Counsellor
Counselled young people with a variety of problems centring on homelessness. Managed a heavy caseload, giving advice and information on housing and benefit entitlements where appropriate, and participated in supervision and support meetings. Attended residential course on Means-tested Benefits by the Welfare Rights Unit.

Example 4

Peel Supplies Ltd
2008 to present
Warehouse and Distribution Supervisor

- Supervised 25 full-time staff, rising to 35 at peak periods
- Instructed and monitored incoming trainees
- Verified and processed orders
- Introduced and established incentive scheme that reduced petty pilfering by 75%
- Promoted from Warehouse Assistant to Warehouse and Distribution Supervisor in 2003

Example 5

Eight 'til Late Shop, Bartonbury
2007 to 2011
Cashier and Kiosk Assistant
General care of stock:

- Checked deliveries
- Replenished shelves
- Ordered stock using computerised system

Cash handling:

- Cashier duties, including balancing tills
- Handled upwards of £5,000 per day

Customer care:

- Served and assisted customers
- Handled enquiries and complaints
- Responsible for alcohol and cigarette legislation

Example 6

The Woodland School Project, Bannham
Summer 2006 and 2008
Drama Instructor
Worked as part of a team to plan and implement out-of-school drama project for 70 mixed-ability students aged 8 to 11. Taught performance techniques, monitored students' progress, maintained records. Coached and motivated to production standard, set goals to encourage performance levels.

Section 5 – your education and training

If you have just left school, college or university, this section will probably take a higher priority and include more detailed information. If, however, you have more than two years' experience of working, your career details will be of more interest to a prospective employer.

Education and training can include:

- academic achievements, diplomas and degrees, etc;
- professional qualifications;

- technical qualifications;
- vocational training where relevant;
- relevant company training programmes;
- computer skills and training;
- language skills;
- professional membership of relevant associations.

Start with the highest, most recent *or* most relevant qualification, give the name of school, college or university, the dates you attended, and the qualification you achieved. You could also include brief details of what was covered in the course, especially if you are recently qualified.

Don't forget to include details of any professional training you have, including training undertaken at work and the qualifications and skills you attained.

Example 1

West Midlands University
2008 to 2011
BSc Computer Science

- Robotics – concepts, VAL, 3-D modelling of component assembly, matrices
- Graphics – 2-D and 3-D, projection, transformation matrices
- Communications – network theory, protocols, hardware
- Database Theory – structure storage, design
- Formal Logic – trinary, fuzzy, temporal
- Artificial Intelligence – Popll, expert systems, Prolog, theory of neural nets

Example 2

2002 University of the South
  Postgraduate Diploma in European Business Administration
2000 Institute of Linguists
  Institute of Linguists Intermediate Diploma in German
1999 UOS School of Business
  RSA Preparatory Certificate Teaching English as a Foreign Language
1998 London University
  BA Hons English and German Literature 2:1

Example 3

2000–2005 Westbrook College of Further Education
 Certificate of Counselling Theory AEB/CAC
 Certificate of Counselling Practice AEB/CAC

1997–2000 Forest Community College
 Open Access vocational courses:

- Post-trauma Stress and Critical Incident Debriefing

- Primary Health Care Counselling

- Managing Short-term Counselling Work within Primary Care

- Women and Mental Health

Example 4

Professional qualifications

2008	Diploma in Marketing	Institute of Marketing
2005	Certified Diploma in Accounting and Finance	Chartered Association of Accountants
1998	Diploma in Management Studies	Westland College
1996	BSc Hons Degree Economics	University of Dorset

Professional training

Computer skills
 Microsoft Office Suite:
  Word
  Access
  Excel
  PowerPoint
  Outlook

Language skills
 Fluent conversational and business German
 Competent spoken French

Member of the Institute of Marketing

Example 5

1996 to 1999 Collworth College of Technology
BTEC HND Food Technology
Access to Science Course

1991 to 1996 Albert Ellis High School
3 A levels: Economics, French, English
5 GCSEs including Maths and English

Section 6 – your personal details

The details covered in this section include the following:

Personal details:

- date of birth, if you wish to include it;
- possession of a clean driving licence;
- nationality – if relevant;
- special details such as a registered disability.

Interests and activities:

brief details of anything that will add to or support the picture of yourself you are presenting.

References:

usually covered by 'available on request'.

Example 1

Date of birth:	15 November 1980
Driver:	Car owner, full, clean UK licence
Interests:	Team sports – netball, volleyball. Running. Took part in London Marathon in 2008
References:	Available on request

Example 2

Date of birth:	25 May 1961
Driving licence:	Full, clean UK licence
Health:	Non-smoker
Interests:	All aspects of conservation work including the National Trust for Conservation, World Wide Fund for Nature, and the RSPB. Chair of the local conservation group, and have organised and participated in several local projects.
References:	Available on request.

Your CV should look something like the following when you've finished.

William Edwards
5 Holton Green Road
Stowerbridge
Lancs LN 4 6TD

Tel: 00000 000000
E-mail: willedwards@anyisp.com

CAREER PROFILE

Key strengths

KEY SKILLS

- Managing accounts and maintaining long-term customer relationships
- Motivating, developing and recruiting staff, including staff training and incentives
- Planning and controlling sales resources to maximum effect
- Maintaining cash flow and profitability
- Analysing and evaluating sales results
- Planning and implementing public relations and advertising campaigns

CAREER HISTORY

Sullivan Centres
2006 to present
Area Manager
Managed Northern region of a national charity:

- Increased funding revenue by 57% over three years
- Took over and re-established area that had fallen into neglect
- Built up team of trained, professional volunteers
- Established efficient collection service
- Produced and implemented marketing plan
- Improved methods of forwarding donations
- Worked towards Institute of Management NVQ level 4

EJK & Sons Ltd
2002 to 2006
Sales/Product Manager
Directly responsible to the Managing Director and Sales and Marketing
Director for all aspects relating to promotion and sale of product range:

- Organised and established new product range from concept to
  completion
- Took over two neglected product ranges and increased turnover by
  37%
- Organised continuous training programme for internal and external
  sales personnel with training in sales and product knowledge
- Planned and organised exhibitions and seminars
- Prepared and delivered presentations at all levels including hands-on
  product demonstrations to groups of all sizes

Utilities (UK) Ltd
1997 to 2002
Product Manager

- Successfully increased sales year on year
- Maintained profitability of product range
- Organised consistently innovative public relations and advertising
  campaign
- Introduced and marketed new product ranges
- Trained and managed sales team
- Supervised customer orders and oversaw stock control

Bearstrom Ltd
1993 to 1997
Sales Manager, Sales Representative

- Increased sales turnover
- Introduced new products and marketing ideas
- Recruited and trained sales team
- Promoted to Sales Manager in 1995

EDUCATION

Institute of Management
2009 to 2011
NVQ Sales and Marketing Management level 4

City Community School
1986 to 1993
　A levels: Mathematics; Geography
　GCSEs: seven including Maths and English

PERSONAL DETAILS

Date of birth:	4 May 1975
Health:	non-smoker
Interests:	Badminton, riding, coach for under-11 football team

Full, clean UK driving licence

References available on request

Any questions?

What if I don't have any achievements?

Does it help to think of them as accomplishments rather than achievements? In every job you've held, you must have accomplished something, had some goal or outcome in mind, otherwise why bother turning up for work each day? Even the most routine jobs offer the chance to learn new skills, interact with others, meet targets, improve your working methods and develop new responsibilities. Read some of the CVs later in this book to give you some ideas and get you thinking.

What if there are gaps in my work record?

If the gaps include voluntary work, training or relevant experience – travel, for example – put these down as part of your skills, qualifications and achievements. Otherwise, giving the year of employment, rather than month and year, will cover short employment gaps.

Example

Change this ...	*... to this*
Career history	Career history
Sollbury Ltd	Sollbury Ltd
September 2010 to July 2011	2010 to 2011
Market researcher	**Market researcher**
Hunt and Covey Retail	Hunt and Covey Retail
August 2008 to January 2010	2008 to 2010
Retail Assistant	Retail Assistant

If the gaps are early on in your career history, focus attention on your current position, and very briefly summarise that period of employment:

Various
1999 to 2004
Retail and market research

For solutions to other CV problems, see Chapter 6.

Chapter Three
The tailor-made CV

If you were beginning to wonder what to do with those first two sections on your CV – the Career profile and Key strengths – this is the chapter that lets you in on the secret. They are your opportunity to tailor your CV so that each application you make addresses the specific needs and requirements of that employer.

Why would you want to do that?

Recruitment these days is a matter of competency and fit. Companies go to great lengths to establish the competencies required for each job; that is, the knowledge, skills, personal qualities and experience that mean that you will be able to do that job. When a vacancy is advertised, the ad is based on those core competencies. When the CVs come in, companies look at applicants to see if they are a good fit – how well does what's being offered match what they've said they want? Candidates with the CVs that demonstrate the best fit are the ones who are picked for interview.

There will be dozens, there could even be hundreds, of people applying for the same job you are – all with roughly the same background and experience as you. You need to stand out, and to make your CV stand out you need to offer the best fit possible. A sure-fire way to do so is to write your Career profile and your Key strengths sections afresh each time so that they reflect *precisely* the *exact* requirements of the job.

Read the job ad

Many job advertisements will tell you exactly what to put in your CV. Study the following ad, for example.

Personal Assistant

A small private publisher urgently requires a mature, hard-working assistant to provide administrative and secretarial support. Must have excellent communication and organisational abilities. Keyboard skills (Microsoft Office suite currently used) and a confident telephone manner essential. Experienced bookkeeper familiar with spreadsheets would be an advantage but training will be given to the right applicant. Understanding of environmental issues desirable. Must be able to work on own initiative without supervision and have a flexible approach to working hours.

What is the purpose of the job?

To provide secretarial, administrative and organisational support to a small private publisher (probably concerned with environmental issues), including bookkeeping and answering the phone.

What is the value of the job to the company?

Competent, efficient administrative support ensures that the publisher can do their job unhindered; a professional face is presented to the world (preparing letters and answering the phone); business records and data are organised, which means they can be accessed, retrieved and used easily.

What are the crucial competencies? (Skills, knowledge, qualifications, experience?)

Computer skills – preferably Microsoft Office; secretarial and admin experience; communication skills including confident phone manner; organisational abilities; initiative, ie the ability to plan and prioritise.

What are the desirable competencies?

Some bookkeeping experience; familiarity with spreadsheets (Excel if they use Microsoft Office); *or* someone able and willing to undergo training; an understanding of environmental issues.

What sort of person are they looking for?

Someone with a confident, mature, professional attitude; self-motivated and experienced enough to work on their own initiative without constant supervision; willing to learn new skills; interested in the environment; flexible (not a 9-to-5 person). Someone used to routine office work but able to cope with responsibility and the unexpected when it arises.

Now take an ad for a job you'd like to apply for and go through it asking yourself the same questions. It helps to write down the answers – don't try to keep them all in your head: you need to be able to look at them to do the next bit.

Use the information to customise your CV

The first thing to ask yourself is: is this the sort of job I want, and do I have these particular skills and qualities? If the answer's yes, complete the remaining two sections on your CV: the Career profile and Key strengths.

Career profile

Use the information to write a Career profile that emphasises just how good a fit your current situation, background and future requirements are with the company you are applying to.

A Career profile is a short statement that gives a summary of who you are, what you do and what you are aiming for with your application. It needs to be as succinct as possible while including:

- who you are – your job title, professional status and background;
- what you can offer – your skills, experience and knowledge;
- what you've achieved – what you most want the employer to know about you, and the unique combination of skills, knowledge and experience that makes you right for this job;
- what you want next – the role you want and why, the sort of company you want to work for and the opportunities you would relish.

This Career profile was written to reflect the requirements of the job ad we've just looked at.

The applicant has thought about which aspects of her background and experience would be most relevant and tailored her Career profile accordingly:

CAREER PROFILE

Highly **experienced and reliable** Personal Assistant with **full Microsoft Office training**, current experience of working in an exceptionally busy office and a background in customer relations. Now looking for a position where a **wide spectrum of secretarial, administrative and organisational skills** can be used to the full, providing comprehensive support for a **worthwhile organisation**.

Key strengths

In this section you need to demonstrate that you have exactly the competencies – the skills, personal qualities, knowledge and experience – that the company requires. It's a simple matter of looking at what they want and telling them what you've got. You need to support your statements, though. It's not enough to say you have a particular skill, quality or knowledge; you have to back it up with evidence. Keep your statements short and succinct and tailor them to fit the job you are applying for.

This Key strengths section was written to reflect the requirements of the same job ad:

KEY STRENGTHS

Excellent IT and secretarial skills: four years' secretarial experience providing support for two department heads and an Assistant Director. College trained and fully proficient in Microsoft Office; including Word and Excel; currently using Windows XP.

Communication skills: as PA to Assistant Director, excellent presentation required, both verbal and written, as is the ability to liaise effectively with clients and other members of staff in person, by letter and over the phone. As customer relations clerk, handled incoming calls courteously, diplomatically and efficiently.

Initiative and flexibility: currently required to prioritise own workload and manage day-to-day administrative organisation effectively. Sales drives and conferences mean working competently and resourcefully under pressure to tight deadlines to meet urgent requirements. Always happy to 'go the extra mile' when necessary.

If you'd written that job ad for a Personal Assistant, how could you *not* interview this applicant? Note that she doesn't claim to have bookkeeping experience, although she has been trained to use Excel, a spreadsheet program; nor does she labour her understanding of environmental issues, although she will put in her Personal details that she is a member of the local conservation group and will also include this information in her covering letter. If she had a strong understanding – held an appropriate degree or was actively involved in environmental issues – this information might have been put in her Key strengths section. If an understanding had been essential rather than desirable, details would *have* to be there.

Emphasising your good fit by highlighting it in a separate section like this saves the employer the effort of having to search out the information from the rest of your CV. Some competencies are very specific, anyway. Would you go into detail about your ability to 'put clients at their ease' or 'build reciprocal customer relationships' in a non-tailored CV? Yet if that's what the employer is asking for, that's what you need to give them.

The rest of your CV

The rest of your CV needs to support everything you've said in these two sections. After completing them, check over the rest of your CV to see if it needs strengthening in any way. Are there other duties or responsibilities that would be appropriate for the job you're applying for? Are there irrelevancies that could be taken out? Do you have relevant achievements that should be mentioned to support your Career profile and Key strengths?

Go back through the job ad. Is there any information there that you haven't used? Any skills, qualities or experience you haven't mentioned? Any personal characteristics you haven't talked about? If you went through the ad with a red pen and crossed out every word and phrase you've addressed, just about all that should be left is the odd 'and' and 'the'.

William Edwards's completed tailor-made CV will follow shortly. First, here's the job ad it was written for. He's underlined three of the essential attributes the successful candidate will have and you'll see afterwards how he uses them to write his Key strengths section.

Fundraising Director, International Medical Charity

We are looking for a Fundraising Director to join a dynamic team concerned with raising money for an internationally recognised medical charity. This is a hands-on role whose purpose is to lead and manage the fundraising team, effectively generating income from major donors, private individuals, trusts, foundations and businesses in the UK and internationally.

The successful candidate will have <u>strong leadership skills</u> and a <u>track record in Fundraising</u> or Sales/Marketing with the emphasis on face-to-face income generation along with team leadership and management. Applicants should be able to generate income through relationship creation, development and <u>excellent presentation</u>. You should be willing to travel within the UK and abroad.

If you feel you meet these criteria, please send your CV to Irene Lowel at _____.

William has taken his prepared CV on pages 25–27 and completed the first two sections – his Career profile and Key strengths – using the information in the job ad to focus his ideas.

William Edwards
5 Holton Green Road
Stowerbridge
Lancs LN 4 6TD

Tel: 00000 000000
E-mail: willedwards@anyisp.com

Career profile

Area Manager with a major UK charity with a professional background in sales and marketing. Solid experience of fundraising, working with trusts and foundations as well as businesses and individuals, and of training and motivating a highly successful team to achieve unprecedented results. Now looking for a role where knowledge and understanding of the business of charity can be used to good effect.

Key strengths

Successful track record in fundraising: six years' experience of upgrading a neglected, underperforming area into a major contributor with a 57 per cent increase in funding based on substantial relationship-building skills developed over more than a decade in sales and marketing.

Presentation skills: currently required to give effective yet enjoyable talks and presentations to the public, the media and other interested bodies to raise awareness and secure donations. Donations last year totalled £3.5 million.

Strong leadership skills: a track record of over 10 years of motivating teams to set and achieve challenging targets and expect the very best from themselves. Feedback from teams demonstrates a vigorous style of leadership based on sincere consultation allied with clear direction and a solid understanding of marketing techniques.

Key skills

- Maintaining long-term customer relationships
- Motivating, developing and recruiting staff, including staff training and incentives
- Planning and controlling resources to maximum effect
- Maintaining cash flow and profitability
- Analysing and evaluating results
- Planning and implementing public relations and advertising campaigns

Career history

Sullivan Centres
2006 to present
Area Manager
Managed Northern region of a national charity:

- Increased funding revenue by 57% over three years
- Took over and re-established area that had fallen into neglect
- Built up team of trained, professional volunteers
- Established efficient collection service
- Produced and implemented marketing plan
- Improved methods of forwarding donations
- Worked towards Institute of Management NVQ level 4

EJK & Sons Ltd
2002 to 2006
Sales/Product Manager
Directly responsible to the Managing Director and Sales and Marketing Director for all aspects relating to promotion and sale of product range:

- Organised and established new product range from concept to completion
- Took over two neglected product ranges and increased turnover by 37%
- Organised continuous training programme for internal and external sales personnel with training in sales and product knowledge
- Planned and organised exhibitions and seminars
- Prepared and delivered presentations at all levels, including hands-on product demonstrations to groups of all sizes

Utilities (UK) Ltd
1997 to 2002
Product Manager

- Successfully increased sales year on year
- Maintained profitability of product range
- Organised consistently innovative public relations and advertising campaigns
- Introduced and marketed new product ranges
- Trained and managed sales team
- Supervised customer orders and oversaw stock control

Bearstrom Ltd
1993 to 1997
Sales Manager, Sales Representative

- Increased sales turnover
- Introduced new products and marketing ideas
- Recruited and trained sales team
- Promoted to Sales Manager in 1995

Education

Institute of Management, 2009 to 2011
  NVQ Sales and Marketing Management level 4
City Community School, 1986 to 1993
  A levels: Mathematics; Geography
  GCSEs: seven including Maths and English

Personal details

Date of birth:	4 May 1975
Health:	non-smoker
Interests:	Badminton, riding, coach for under-11 football team

Full, clean UK driving licence

References available on request

Look for other information

While you're customising your CV, look around for any other background information you can find about the job and the company. Knowledge is power, and the more you know, the more empowered you become.

The job description

Quite often, ads ask you to contact the company for more information. Always do so, because it will often send you useful things like company information and a comprehensive job description for the vacancy. This will give you even more detail about the duties and responsibilities of the job and the required competencies.

The company website

Look up the company home page on the internet for information about the sort of company it is: what it does, what sort of image it has, what sort of clients it has and so on. As well as straightforward factual information, get as much of a feel for the company as you can.

Annual reports and company brochures

Most companies will send copies of these to you if you ask.

Articles

Put the company name into a search engine to see what comes up.

Professional profiles

Look up the sort of job you want on career sites and on professional association sites and chat rooms. These can give you an overview of the key requirements and alert you to what the current issues are.

More examples

Each of the following Career profiles was written with a specific job and company in mind, using information from the job ad and the other sources outlined above.

- A professional and highly skilled Retail Manager with six years' experience in high-street retail and a thorough understanding of how to maximise turnover through stock rotation and P&L monitoring. A sales professional with a sound commitment to customer focus and the management skills needed to motivate a sales team to exceed sales targets three years running. Now looking for a position with a recognised leader in the field where these skills can be used to achieve quality results and the highest level of customer satisfaction.

- Youth Worker with NVQ level 4 in Advice and Guidance and four years' experience in the community working face-to-face with young people, helping them to overcome social and economic disadvantages. As someone passionate about diversity and inclusion, I am currently seeking a similarly challenging role where I can make full use of my skills and practical experience to help service users solve problems, overcome barriers and implement effective solutions.

- A highly experienced, MBA-qualified Export Manager with eight years' track record of success in export sales, providing high-quality solutions to technical problems and achieving a 27 per cent growth in sales over three years. With a background in engineering and experience of selling into several industry sectors including telecommunications, I am currently interested in a decision-making role with a leading-edge organisation offering the opportunity to further develop excellent management skills and contribute to company growth.

- Office Supervisor with four years' experience of organising data and records and the tried and tested ability to maintain a consistently high standard of work and attention to detail under pressure, and to motivate staff to do the same. I am now looking for a challenging work environment where recently updated and enhanced computer skills can be put to good use ensuring the efficient working of a busy and demanding department.

- Graphic Designer with HND, three years' experience and first-rate skills in using OSX, Creative Suite 3, Photoshop and Illustrator. Experienced at taking client briefs through to finished artwork, including brochures, advertising and point-of-sale material, and member of the team that won the Indesign Pro award this year. Now looking for the opportunity to join a fast-moving, highly skilled team working on some of the world's most exciting brand names.

Any questions?

What if there isn't enough information in the job ad?

By the time you've applied for several jobs, you'll probably find that you're putting some Key strengths in most of the time. When an ad doesn't give much more than a job title and asks you to apply, these are the Key strengths to use. Find out what you can about the company and make use of the information sources we looked at above, and use your intuition and job knowledge to deduce what other strengths they might need, or look at the requirements for a range of jobs with the same or similar job title on a recruitment site such as monster.co.uk.

What if I'm not applying for an advertised vacancy?

If you're making speculative approaches – sending your CV to companies that haven't yet advertised a vacancy – then use the same techniques as above. Customise your Career profile to suit the company you're approaching and use your knowledge and experience to work out what skills and qualities they would most value.

If you're posting your CV on a recruitment site or sending out a mass CV mailing, then either decide what sort of company you want to work for and put that in your Career profile, or leave that part out altogether and just focus on who you are and what you've done.

I've looked at the job description and it lists 10 competencies. Do I have to address all of them?

Pick out the two or three that make this job different from all the others and put these in your Key strengths section, or pick the ones you know to be the most valuable and sought-after. Mention the others in your Key skills or under 'Achievements' in your work history, but make sure that they go in somewhere.

Why do I have to customise my CV; can't all this go in my covering letter?

Yes, it can go in your covering letter and it should, but it needs to go in your CV as well. Use your covering letter to say why you are applying for this particular job with this particular company and point out what a good match your skills and experience are for the requirements of the job. Use the same sources that you used to customise your CV but don't just repeat the information: rephrase it and try to come up with a fresh angle. We'll look at all this in more detail in the next chapter.

However, your covering letter can become detached from your CV; your CV can be filed without the letter; your CV can be scanned into a bank minus the letter; your CV can be passed on to HR or a department head without the letter... better by far to have the most important information – your suitability for the job – actually on your CV, where there is no chance it can get lost or be overlooked.

Chapter Four
Covering letters

Never underestimate the power of your covering letter. A well thought-out letter or e-mail will:

- highlight your key attributes at a glance;
- emphasise your excellent match to the job requirements;
- direct attention to your good points, and away from any weaker ones;
- reinforce the professional impression you want to create;
- get your CV read with attention.

Writing letters

Your covering letter is the first impression an employer gets of you, and a letter that makes a *good* first impression ensures your CV is read with just that little bit more interest and attention. Any letter you write has five key objectives. You need to do the following.

1. Make a favourable impression

As your letter is your first contact with the company, the impact you make at this stage will have an important effect on what happens next. Don't wait until the interview to make a good impression; you may never get that opportunity.

2. Inform

A good covering letter presents the most important points from your CV or application form. It should highlight the key details about your skills and experience that are most relevant to the job, clearly and succinctly.

3. Persuade

Your chosen details, along with the style and tone of your letter, should persuade the reader of your professionalism and suit-ability for the position, and encourage them to consider you further.

4. Secure attention

Letters must be interesting enough for the reader to want to know more, but shouldn't attempt to say everything – this is what the rest of your CV and, with luck, the interview are for.

5. Build a good relationship

Put thought into building a good relationship with the people you write to. Use the tone and style of your letter to create a friendly, professional impression. Consider using follow-up and thank you letters to develop further goodwill.

Time spent crafting a great letter is never wasted. When you have a good one, you can adapt it for use again and again.

Making a good impression

Letters must be short, succinct and, above all, relevant. They should look professional and be easy to read, which means paying atten-tion to the appearance, layout, readability and content.

Appearance

- Use plain, unlined white or cream A4 paper, preferably 100 gsm weight, and use one side of the paper only.

- Print it in a style and typeface that match your CV unless, very rarely, a handwritten letter is asked for specifically.

- Check and double-check grammar and spelling.

- Sent your letter and CV unfolded in a plain, white or cream envelope.

- As you are always going to send your letter to a named individual and tailor it specifically to their requirements, there is no need to tell you to print the letter out afresh each time you apply for a job and never send a photocopy.

Layout

Use a standard business layout like the ones shown in the example letters in this chapter.

Readability

- Use a plain, clear 11- or 12-point typeface.

- Keep it concise; one page should be enough.

- Keep sentences and paragraphs short. Two short paragraphs are better than one long one.

- Dense blocks of text are hard to read.

- Make the main points clear. Covering letters are skimmed through rather than read, so, even though it's a letter, use bullet points to emphasise your:

  - key strengths;

  - specific skills;

  - main achievements.

- Include enough white space to make it look easy to read and inviting – use wide margins and clear paragraph breaks.

Content

Write to a named individual, not 'Dear Sir or Madam', and tailor each letter to relate it to the job you are applying for. Remember that you need to engage the reader's attention and hold their interest. Use the job ad as a guide and demonstrate how well you match the requirements.

Four important paragraphs

Your letter has four distinct parts, four important paragraphs in which to interest, persuade, inform and impress the reader.

Paragraph one

Say why you are writing. If it's in reply to an advertised vacancy, include the title of the job you are applying for and where you saw the advertisement. If it's a speculative letter, start with a brief, topical and relevant paragraph giving your reason for writing.

Examples

I am writing to apply for the position of Personal Assistant as advertised in today's *Evening Post.* Ref: 16K Project Manager.

I am writing to apply for the above post as advertised in this month's issue of *Engineering Times.*

I learnt with interest of your company's plans to open a new branch in Anytown in yesterday's *Evening Chronicle.*

I read with interest on the current *Engineering Today* website about your new contract to manufacture XYZ engineering systems.

It was very nice to meet you at the recent 'Business Today' exhibition and hear about the new developments at your company.

Paragraph two

This is the persuasive part that tells them what you can contribute to the company. Include your relevant skills, experience and especially your achievements. If it's a speculative letter, mention the sort of job you are interested in. You can split this section into two or three short paragraphs if it makes it easier to read. You can also use bullet points if that makes the message clearer.

Examples

- I have been IT Manager at XYZ Ltd for three years and have experience of large-scale software changeover, having restructured the finance department during that time. The problems I've effectively handled include:
  - maintaining turn-around rate during departmental change;
  - designing effective training manuals;
  - taking staff successfully through the change process.
- As you will see from my CV, I have worked on an extensive range of accounts including consumer, recruitment and financial. I have wide experience of creating exciting and imaginative publicity campaigns.
  Of particular interest to you will be the XYZ campaign, a copy of which I enclose. This prompted a response rate of 22%, the highest ever achieved by the agency.
- Among the skills that will be of most interest to you are:
  - excellent staff management;
  - a first-rate record in administration;
  - proficiency at prioritising workloads;
  - the ability to implement standard procedures efficiently.
- My recent achievements include organising and supervising staff training to introduce Microsoft Office as standard across the board. This resulted in a significant increase in both departmental and interdepartmental efficiency.

Paragraph three

Use this section to say why you are applying for the job. Make your reason positive and persuasive, emphasising what you can bring to the new position, rather than what you hope they'll do for you. Good reasons for changing your job include:

- opportunity – the chance to develop or do something new;
- challenge – more demanding responsibilities;

- promotion – the job you're applying for is a step up from your current one;

- reputation – applying to a more prestigious company.

There are other reasons for changing jobs that are just as valid but somewhat harder to defend in a covering letter. They are:

- money – your salary no longer reflects your value;

- security – you would like a more secure job with a more stable company;

- location – the company you're applying to is in a better or more convenient place.

Whatever reason you give, never criticise your current employer. Say that you enjoy your current job then explain why, nevertheless, you want to change.

Examples

- I am presently working at the marketing organisation XYZ. However, I would very much like to return to production, where I feel my skills and experience could be used more effectively, and would welcome the opportunity this position offers to do so.

- I have enjoyed working at XYZ, and have welcomed the chance this has given me to cultivate my administrative skills. I am now, however, looking for a post with more responsibility, and feel that your advertisement offers the opportunity I am looking for.

- I am keen to find an organisation offering continued training and development, and the chance to progress in this area. I am, in consequence, very interested in the vacancy you have to offer.

Paragraph four

This should be a short paragraph to close the letter, confirming your interest in the job.

Examples

I would welcome the opportunity to discuss my application with you further, and look forward to hearing from you.

I would be very happy to discuss my application with you in more detail, and look forward to hearing from you.

I would really appreciate the opportunity of a short meeting to discuss possible openings within your organisation, and will contact your office within the next few days to request a convenient date and time.

Six useful letters

The most useful letters in your job search are:

- the covering letter you send with your CV in answer to an advertised vacancy;
- the speculative letter you send with your CV to an employer who might have a suitable opening for you;
- the networking letter asking for help and advice;
- the follow-up letter you send after an interview, underlining your interest and suitability;
- the update letter reminding companies who you are and what you can offer;
- the pared-down e-mail that secures online attention.

Here are examples of each of them, with two covering letters for an advertised vacancy because this is the one you will probably use most.

Covering letter for an advertised vacancy – Example 1

1 Yourstreet
Yourtown
Yourcounty AA0 0AA
Tel: 00000 000000
Mobile: 00000 000000
E-mail: name@anyisp.co.uk

1 January 2012

Jane Smith
Personnel Manager
XYZ Ltd
111 Anystreet
Anytown AA0 0AA

Re: Marketing Manager Ref 34 WT

Dear Ms Smith,

I am writing to apply for the position of Marketing Manager as advertised in this month's *Retail Direct*.

As you will see from my CV, I have extensive marketing experience, including three years with ABC Ltd. I have a particular interest in product planning, having successfully researched and implemented market strategy for several profitable new product lines including Glascon and Intex.

Currently, I am Department Leader at DEF & Co, the product research organisation. I would, however, prefer to return to consumer marketing as I believe this is where my skills and experience can be used most effectively. I am consequently very interested in the opportunity your vacancy offers.

I would be very happy to discuss my application with you in more detail, and look forward to hearing from you in the near future.

Yours sincerely

(Signature)

John Brown
Enc. CV

Covering letter for an advertised vacancy – Example 2

1 Yourstreet
Yourtown
Yourcounty AA0 0AA
Tel: 00000 000000
Mobile: 00000 000000
E-mail: name@anyisp.co.uk

1 January 2012

Jane Smith
Personnel Manager
XYZ Ltd
111 Anystreet
Anytown AA0 0AA

Dear Ms Smith,

I am writing to apply for the position of Personal Assistant as advertised in this week's *Daily Advertiser.*

I believe I have the skills and qualities that you are asking for. I have five years' secretarial and administrative experience requiring excellent keyboard skills, and a confident telephone manner developed through extensive experience in customer services.

My current position is with McDonald Partners, where I am personal assistant to the senior partner, responsible for the organisation and administration of the office. My responsibilities include:

- organising the everyday running of the office including word processing letters and reports, using Microsoft Word, Excel, and Outlook Express;
- dealing with enquiries from the public and other departments;
- scheduling appointments and planning and organising meetings;
- liaising with colleagues to ensure the smooth running of the department.

While my work at ABC has been very enjoyable, I also have a keen awareness of environmental issues, being an active member of the Conservation Trust. Hence my interest in the job that you are offering.

I would be very happy to discuss my application with you in more detail and look forward to hearing from you in the near future.

Yours sincerely

(Signature)

Jane Brown
Enc. CV

Speculative letter

1 Yourstreet
Yourtown
Yourcounty AA0 0AA
Tel: 00000 000000
Mobile: 00000 000000
E-mail: name@anyisp.co.uk

1 January 2012

Jane Smith
Personnel Manager
XYZ Ltd
111 Anystreet
Anytown AA0 0AA

Dear Ms Smith,

I was interested to read of the new education initiatives for the area outlined in today's *Evening Post*, and wonder if you have an opening for an adult literacy and numeracy teacher with counselling qualifications.

As you will see from my CV, I have considerable experience of working with people from a variety of backgrounds. I have been involved with the adult literacy scheme at the ABC Centre since its opening in 2009, as a tutor and student adviser, and I also work as a volunteer counsellor with the DEF Trust.

I have City & Guilds qualifications in both Basic Education Teaching and Practical Counselling. In addition, I have attended GHI College's Planned Adult Literacy Course and undergone counselling training with DEF Trust.

As the current project at the ABC Centre is drawing to a close, I am eager to continue to develop my career and make full use of my skills and experience where they would be of value. I believe your organisation could offer the opportunity to do so.

I would really appreciate the chance to discuss any suitable positions with you in more detail, and look forward to hearing from you in the near future.

Yours sincerely

(Signature)

John Brown
Enc. CV

Networking letter

43 East Parade
Oxhill
Devon DV3 9EJ
Tel: 00000 000000
e-mail: name@anyisp.co.uk

25 April 2012

Nell Sandiman
St Lawrence Associates
St Lawrence
Devon DV6 8TH

Dear Ms Sandiman,

I am writing to you as a fellow member of the Finance Circle to ask for your advice. As you will have heard, the recent merger between Lang International and General Finance has caused major upheavals. Sadly, the department where I have worked for the past three years is to close at the end of the year. While the company has offered me the opportunity to work with them on a freelance basis, I would prefer something with more stability.

As an executive with a broad background in financial administration, I am now looking for a permanent position within the field. My 15 years' experience in finance includes five years in the design and implementation of accounting and management systems, and six years in accounts and data-processing.

I wonder, therefore, if you know of any likely opening for someone with my skills and experience, or if you could recommend any friends, associates or business contacts who it could be worth my while talking to?

I look forward to hearing from you, and I would greatly appreciate any information or advice that you can give me.

Yours sincerely

(Signature)

Henry Gilby

Follow-up letter

53 Hillcroft Avenue
St Agnes Hill
Norwich NR11 6LM
Tel: 00000 000000
e-mail: name@anyisp.co.uk

2 March 2012

Ms Alice N Murray
Personnel Manager
St Agnes Patient Services Trust
St Agnes
Norwich NR7 7SS

Dear Ms Murray,

Thank you for interviewing me for the post of Outpatient Transport Service Driver yesterday, Monday 1 March 2012. I greatly appreciated the opportunity to meet you.

During the interview I felt I gained a deeper understanding of the responsibilities of the job. It was very interesting to see in more detail how the Outpatient Transport Service fits into the wider picture of patient care.

I believe that this is exactly the sort of position that I am looking for, and I hope that you consider that I have the character and experience necessary to make a useful contribution.

I look forward to hearing from you.

Yours sincerely

(Signature)

Robert Catskill

Update letter

12 Henshaw Crescent
Upper Tithing
Northamptonshire NP18 6AL
Tel: 00000 000000
e-mail: name@anyisp.co.uk

30 April 2012

Mrs Julia Crabb
Department Head
Rex Gambler
Hills Barton
Northamptonshire NP7 7HB

Dear Mrs Crabb,

I wrote to you in March regarding the possibility of openings for office personnel with your company. The conversation that we had at that time was most interesting and informative, and gave me a good insight into the organisation. I am now writing to you again to see if any opportunities have arisen in the meantime.

Since our conversation I have further upgraded my skills with an accounting course using the Addition Accountant system. This included modules on sales, purchases and nominal ledgers, producing reports, audit trails and VAT procedures, among others.

I have enclosed an updated CV giving full details of this as well as my background and experience to date.

I would very much welcome the opportunity to talk to you again to see how things have developed during the past six months. I will call your office during the next week to see if a short discussion about the current situation would be possible.

Yours sincerely

(Signature)

Vita Sharp
Enc. CV

E-mail

Any of these letters can, of course, be sent as an e-mail; the contents will be exactly the same. The only difference is the form the letter takes – e-mails need to be pared down so that the really important information hits the middle of the screen when the e-mail is opened. Keep in mind that:

- the screen is smaller than an A4 letter;
- e-mail is often read more quickly and with less attention;
- your e-mail is competing for attention with many others;
- your e-mail may need to be sent on or forwarded;
- your CV and covering letter may initially be scanned by software rather than a person.

This means that:

- you have only a small window of opportunity in which to persuade the recruiter to go on and read your CV;
- every line counts – even the subject line;
- keywords are even more important in e-mailed covering letters than in mailed ones.

Even if you are sending out dozens of identical e-mails, send them individually and resist the temptation to copy them to everyone at the same time.

Present your e-mail as well as you would any other letter, and keep your wording professional and businesslike.

Make sure your key points appear on the opening screen and give the reader a good reason to scroll down further.

Example

To: jsmith@abcltd.com
Cc:
Subject: Ref K121 Sales Manager – IT experienced applicant

Dear Ms Smith,

I would like to apply for the position of Senior Project Manager as detailed on salesjobs.com.

I have an excellent track record in Project Management, particularly in Information Technology, having worked for some of the major companies in this field.

My achievements include:

- developing three multi-million pound projects;
- increasing XYZ's penetration of the IT sector by 25%;
- increasing the market share of DEF by 15%;
- increasing XYZ's profits by 11%.

As well as being a skilled communicator, supportive, thorough, innovative and decisive, I also possess practical management skills, having:

- led professional teams on major marketing projects;
- taken overall responsibility for four major product launches;
- formulated policy at all stages of development.

I look forward to discussing my application with you in more detail, and I hope to hear from you in the near future. My full CV follows below, and is also attached as a separate document.

Yours sincerely
Jane Brown
Tel: 00000 000000

Chapter Five
Your online CV

How things have changed

The advances in computer technology and developments in the workplace mean that application procedures have changed in significant ways. In particular, we've seen the increased use of computers to:

- advertise job vacancies on the internet;
- facilitate online job applications;
- provide access to CV banks;
- scan and store CVs in databases;
- scan CVs to pre-select likely candidates.

This means that, these days, a computer-friendly CV is essential for any job seeker.

How the internet can help

One of the key reasons for computer-proofing your CV is so you can get maximum benefit from using the internet. Over the past few years, the internet has become a major job-search tool. This significant means of communication offers the opportunity to:

- obtain information about companies and employers;
- discover the jobs on offer;

- contact potential employers promptly;
- boost the scale and speed of your applications;
- network with newsgroups;
- get your CV in front of many more recruiters;
- post your CV in a variety of CV banks;
- scan job banks;
- find and apply for a wide variety of opportunities.

Other advantages of applying online are:

- Your application arrives in perfect condition.
- It arrives promptly without being delayed in the post.
- It's cheaper – a particular consideration if you're sending lots of applications for jobs abroad.

When you're searching for a job, the internet is probably going to be one of your most useful tools. Like all tools, however, it has its advantages and its drawbacks, so this chapter looks at how you can use your CV to get the best out of the internet and how it can help you get ahead of the competition.

Your CV and the internet

The internet has become increasingly popular for job hunting due to the vast amount of online resources available. At the click of a button you can visit employers' websites to gather useful information, or find professional groups online to network with. But searching for jobs online can take up a lot of time – there are thousands of job boards and recruitment websites. Just typing 'sales manager' or 'accountant' into a search engine will open up an overwhelming number of possibilities, only a handful of which will be relevant to you. You need to be able to keep this flood of information manageable, while not neglecting valuable leads.

There are a number of things that can make your job search easier, more efficient and more effective.

Job boards and CV databanks

Job boards advertise job vacancies placed by employers and recruitment agencies. They range from big, multi-sector ones that have vacancies in all industries, to smaller, specialist job sites dedicated to a particular profession or specialisation. Sites are easy to navigate, allowing you to use keywords and key phrases to narrow your search, and when you find a suitable job the site will give you full instructions about how to apply online or upload your CV.

Don't restrict yourself to just one or two sites – use as many job boards as are appropriate to your circumstances and make full use of any additional services they offer such as job alerts – e-mails that automatically notify you when someone posts a vacancy you might be interested in.

Many job boards will also let you post your CV in their online CV databank so that it's visible to registered recruitment agencies and employers. This service is invaluable: databases are searched by thousands of recruiters – not just every day, but every hour, so adding your CV to an online database means you could be picked for a vacancy you didn't even know existed.

Registration is usually free and you can keep your CV current by updating your profile at any time. Once registered, your CV can be working for you 24 hours a day while you get on with approaching other employers. If you are worried your CV might be noticed online by your current employer, make sure the database you choose has suitable privacy controls.

Check what job boards and databases can offer you in addition to the basics and use every tool that could be of service. Many job sites will let you:

- Set up e-mail alerts for new vacancies that match your profile.

- Store CVs and covering letters online to save time when applying for jobs.

- Keep a record of your applications to help you keep track of them.

- Use and adapt templates for CVs and covering letters.

- Check things like job salary ranges and company profiles to help you make informed decisions.
- Access tips and advice on everything from CVs to interview techniques.
- Join forums and newsgroups for sharing information and experiences.

Some sites also offer, usually for a fee, specialist services such as:

- Job feeds throughout the day, ensuring you hear about new vacancies the moment they arrive.
- Access to expert advice on relevant topics via e-mail.
- Personality profiling and career assessment.
- Interactive interview practice via video.
- CV writing services, career coaching and online training.

Job search engines

These are an easy way of finding specific vacancies online. As their name suggests, they are search engines that browse the big job boards, employers' websites and recruitment agencies' sites in a single search, rather than visiting them individually. When you find something suitable, it will link you directly to the appropriate site.

Recruitment agency websites

Most agencies legitimately post clients' vacancies directly on their websites. Unscrupulous agencies, though, have been known to post non-existent vacancies in order to build up their database of job hunters. If in doubt, phone and find out more before taking it further – it could get very dispiriting if you keep submitting your details and getting no response.

Employers' websites

Most companies use their website for recruitment, and you'll regularly find job vacancies posted there that may never appear anywhere else. Applying directly also demonstrates your interest in the organisation because you were looking at the company site.

Finding sites

To find any of the above just use your main search engine. Put job board, CV database, job search engine, recruitment agencies, company or industry name into it, tailored as you require: 'job board hospitality & catering London', for example, or 'recruitment agencies accounting & finance UK'.

Job sites and databanks are usually free to use – the site is paid by the vacancy advertiser – but you may have to pay a fee for more advanced services such as interview coaching or career assessment.

Your CV online

To get your CV picked out of a database, you need to keep in mind how databases work and how recruiters use them. CVs are screened and selected using keyword scanning – the same way you use keywords to find appropriate sites during your own online browsing.

The importance of keywords

There are thousands of CVs in any online database – the only way yours will get picked is if you include relevant keywords.

These are important in all CVs, but especially so when computerised selection procedures are involved. Any CV needs to grab the reader's attention, but it's even more important when the attention you're trying to grab isn't even human – just a program designed to look for specific words or phrases.

The scanner can't pick out what isn't there, so make your CV easy to find and include those important, specific keywords the scanner is searching for. These are, for example:

- **Positions** – manager, programmer, editor, engineer, director.

- **Occupational background** – teaching, engineering, public relations, retailing, financial management, quality control, customer care, sales and marketing.

- **Knowledge areas** – capacity planning, policy and procedures, interactive technology, systems configuration, project planning, budget and resource management, MIS management, conceptual design, global markets, product development, restructuring, crisis resolution, sales and distribution.

- **Specific skills and qualifications** – Microsoft Word, Windows NT, ISO 9000, BSc, MA, two years' experience of....

- **Workplace skills** – designed, evaluated, represented, organised, formulated, developed.

The keywords in this extract from a CV are highlighted in bold, and the type of keyword is indicated in italics:

Customer Service Manager (*position*)
C&G Telecommunications (*background*) – 2004 to Present
Supervised (*workplace skill*) divisional **customer service** (*background*) staff:

- **Organised** (*workplace skill*) **staff schedules** (*knowledge area*)
- **Trained** (*workplace skill*) staff in **customer care** (*knowledge area*)
- **Implemented** (*workplace skill*) new **policy procedures** (*knowledge area*)
- **Monitored** (*workplace skill*) service to ensure **targets and objectives** (*knowledge area*) met
- Used **Windows XP** (*specific skill*) with **Access** (*specific skill*) for customer **database** (*knowledge area*)

Study the job advertisement or the job description carefully when you compose your CV and extract all the keywords.

Be specific. If the job description asks for word-processing skills, state the specific skills you have – Word, PowerPoint, Outlook, etc. If you are, for example, a manager or a designer, say what you have managed or what you designed.

Go into detail. If you are an IT professional with a range of skills and experience, give details of what exactly those skills and experience are, for instance:

- Four years' experience in IT Development;
- Experience in Unix Operating System;
- Worked as an ORACLE DBA;
- Wrote reports using Report Writer 2x;
- Worked as part of a project team.

Use the CV registration form

When you put a CV onto a database, you usually have to complete a short registration form that includes your current job title, preferred job target and brief information about the sort of work you're looking for. This information is 'tagged' to your CV, so scanners will pick up data included on this, too, giving you another opportunity to include keywords and get your CV in front of potential employers.

Allow for variations

If the most widely used title for your type of job is Media Sales Executive, for example, that's what the scanner will look for, so use standard job titles and/or those used in relevant job vacancy adverts. If in doubt, include alternative job titles in brackets along with any common abbreviations such as CEO for Chief Executive Officer. Apply the same thinking to your qualifications and skills.

Update your CV regularly

Many recruiters limit their search to recently submitted CVs, so keep your CV fresh by resubmitting it regularly. Check, update and refresh it, however minimal the changes, every six to eight weeks. Keep your CV live and active.

Maintain your professional appearance

Whether you are e-mailing your CV directly to an employer or uploading it onto an online CV databank, follow exactly the same rules as you would for any CV:

- Keep it concise.
- Keep it simple so the important information stands out clearly.
- Keep it relevant.
- Make it easy to read.

Even though it's e-mail, this is a formal job application, so:

- no abbreviations, jargon or slang;
- no smiley faces or anything like that;
- start and end formally: Dear Ms Smith ... Yours sincerely.

Sending your CV

You can either send your CV as a file attached to an e-mail, or put it in the main body of the text. Usually, you can send your CV as an attachment, but if the organisation won't accept attached files because of viruses, save your existing word-processed CV as a Rich Text file, then edit and paste it into the e-mail composition box. There's more about how to do this a little later.

- If you're sending your CV as an attached file, include your own name as part of the file name – marysmithcv.doc, for example. It will make it easier to find out of the hundreds of files called cv.doc.
- Don't send large files that will take ages to download. Your CV and covering letter should be ok, but avoid sending large files such as photographs or graphics when contacting an employer online. If they are an important part of your job

application, as might be the case for a graphics portfolio, either send a link to your website, or at least alert the recipient and ask permission before sending.

- Even if you are sending your CV to more than one person or applying for more than one job with the same CV, make sure you send each one as a separate, fresh e-mail. Never, ever cc your CV to several different companies at the same time.

- Check spelling and grammar thoroughly before you click on the send button.

- Get a professional-looking e-mail address – partyanimal@anyisp.co.uk might not be taken seriously.

The subject line

Always fill in the subject line. If you are replying to an advertised vacancy, put the job title and any reference number. If you are making a speculative application, put something appropriate, but make it clear and concise. It may be tempting to try to intrigue with a 'teaser' subject line, but you run the risk of causing irritation when the real purpose of your e-mail becomes clear. Instead, try to include those important keywords:

Subject: Office Manager – City Executive Assistant interested

Subject: Ref 311 Financial Administrator – FCMA 7 years' exp.

Subject: Job ref 2889 – MBA interested

Subject: Marketing exec Ref 446 – New York/London experience offered

Covering letter

Follow with a brief summary of the most important points of your CV – your achievements, skills and experience. Keep in mind that if what appears on the screen doesn't impress, the rest of your e-mail probably won't be read:

Example

Project Manager – IT Experienced
Jane Smith [jsmith@anyisp.com]
To: 'Jane Phillips (jphillips@abc.com)'
Subject: Job ref 771 – IT Project Manager with multi-million pound
        project experience

Dear Ms Phillips,

I would like to apply for the post of Senior Project Manager (Ref 771) as detailed on Jobs.com.

My achievements include:

- developing three multi-million pound projects
- increasing Nestor penetration of IT sector by 15%
- increasing the market share of Highmatch by 10%
- increasing Highmatch profits by 8%

I have an excellent track record in project management, particularly information technology, having worked for major companies in the field.

My full CV follows.

Layout and appearance

Details

Your name, e-mail address and the date already appear at the top of the page. Start the main body of your CV – your Personal Statement followed by your Key Skills/Experience – immediately rather than take up valuable screen space with your home address and telephone number. Put these at the end of your CV instead.

Fonts

Use standard fonts for e-mailed CVs. If you use a font the recipient does not have, your CV could be unreadable.

Screen size

There are 25 lines on that opening e-mail page rather than the 50 or so on a sheet of A4 paper, so there is less opportunity to get key points in. But if you don't fit them into the first screen, the recipient may not bother to scroll down further. Use the opening screen for the key information that will make an employer want to read further.

- Make it as short and concise as possible. A CV that takes up just two A4 pages can run to six or seven on e-mail.

- Arrange information in bite-size – or, rather, screen-size – chunks so that it appears in one easy-to-assimilate piece on-screen.

- Don't rely on formatting tools – bullets, bold, italics and so on. Some recipients will only be able to view e-mail in plain text. Use capital letters and spacing instead to set out the information clearly.

- However, if you know for certain that your recipient can receive HTML format, you can incorporate your CV as it appears in your word-processed copy, complete with bullet points, borders, assorted fonts and the like.

- Get an employer's view of your CV: look at it in the outbox before sending it off.

It is relatively straightforward to adapt your standard CV so that it still looks good even in plain text. The following example shows one that has been changed from formatted to plain text for e-mail.

Changing a CV – an example

Here is an original word-processed CV

Angela Walker
31 Pollard Way
Marsh Cross
Cambridge CM14 2KL

Tel: 00000 000000
e-mail: awalker@anyisp.com

Personal profile

A highly motivated school leaver with experience of office work.
Punctual, reliable and willing to learn, with a good basic education and a
strong aptitude for organisation and administration.

Key skills

- Keyboard skills – 40 wpm
- Operating
  - fax machine
  - photocopiers – Canon and Rank Xerox
  - franking machine
- Preparing and writing routine correspondence
- Organising and carrying out routine administrative work
- Maintaining records
- Dealing with incoming telephone calls
- Dealing with incoming and outgoing mail

Work experience

Summer 2011
Ashbourn & Sedley
Office Assistant

2010–2011
Marsh Cross School Administration Department
Administrative Assistant (part-time/voluntary)

Education

2004–2011 Marsh Cross School
GCSEs

- English language
- English literature
- Maths
- French
- History
- Economics

RSA Stage I Keyboard Skills
RSA Stage I Office Skills
ICT training

Personal details

Date of birth: 30 March 1993
Interests: Riding and pony-trekking, reading and cinema

Here is the same CV, changed to plain text for e-mail:

Office Assistant application
Angela Walker [awalker@anyisp.com]
To: Paul Rogers
Subject: Job ref 58F – school leaver with office experience

Highly motivated school leaver with experience of office work. Punctual, reliable and willing to learn, with a good basic education and a strong aptitude for organisation and administration.

KEY SKILLS

– Keyboard skills – 40wpm

– Fax machine

– Photocopiers – Canon and Rank Xerox

– Franking machine

ADMINISTRATIVE SKILLS
– Preparing and writing routine correspondence
– Organising and performing administrative tasks
– Maintaining records
– Dealing with incoming telephone calls
– Dealing with incoming and outgoing mail

WORK EXPERIENCE
Summer 2011
Ashbourn & Sedley
– Office Assistant
2010–2011
Marsh Cross School Administration Department
– Administrative Assistant (part-time/voluntary)

EDUCATION
2004–2011 Marsh Cross School
GCSE: English language, English literature, Maths, French, History, Economics
RSA Stage I Keyboard Skills
RSA Stage I Office Skills
ICT training

PERSONAL DETAILS
Date of birth: 30 March 1993
Interests: Riding and pony-trekking, reading and cinema
Address: 31 Pollard Way, Marsh Cross, Cambridge CM14 2KL
Tel: 00000 000000

Online application forms

If you reply to an advertised vacancy on an employer's website or recruitment site, the application form may be set up for you already – all you have to do is fill in the blanks. There are drawbacks to ready-prepared application forms, though. They are designed to obtain standard information and don't allow much flexibility about how you present it. If your particular skills and abilities don't stack up neatly in boxes, search out employers who prefer a CV.

Some specific things to remember when you fill in application forms online:

● Read the instructions carefully before you start.

● Don't fill in the application form online and send it off straight away. As with any other application, take time to think about it. You might not have a spellchecker available, so check everything very carefully. Where possible, cut and paste your existing (already spellchecked) plain-text CV into the form to avoid errors.

● Make full use of any hints, tips and advice the site offers. Many offer a considerable amount.

● Fill in all the boxes – incomplete forms are often not accepted.

● As with your CV, make the information you put in as relevant as possible to the job you are applying for.

● Remember to look for and include those keywords.

Paper CVs and scanners

Large organisations that receive many applications often use keyword search software to screen all CVs – even paper-based ones sent to them through the post. If this could affect you, make sure your CV is easily read both by an optical scanner and by scanning software.

When you are mailing your CV:

● Use plain white paper, printed on one side only.

● Use a clear standard 11- or 12-point font.

● Don't staple or paperclip pages together: the second page might not get read.

● Put your name at the top of each page: detached pages can get misplaced.

● Send it unfolded in an A4 envelope: older scanners sometimes try to read fold lines.

- Go easy on bullet points, italics, etc. Revise your CV so it's as plain as possible while still being readable.

- It's vitally important to include the keywords the scanner is searching for.

Online extras

As well as posting your CV on databases and searching job boards, there are other ways you can use the internet to give your job search the edge.

Get your own site

It's possible to design a website or online portfolio for yourself using the facilities now available, even if you have little or no technical skill. A personal site where prospective employers can view your work, read your CV and other relevant information, and obtain your contact details could be an advantage. Put 'free build your own website' into a search engine and see what comes up. Select one that reflects your personality and which creates a professional appearance.

Check your online identity

A positive identity online is becoming important, and becomes increasingly so the further up the career ladder you climb. Put your own name into a search engine and see what comes up. That's exactly what a prospective employer will do when you are being considered for a job.

If you're invisible, you might consider getting a better online presence – joining professional and social networking sites, for example. On the other hand, if what comes up makes you shudder, you might need to do some damage limitation. Make sure that in future things you don't want people to see don't get online.

Network

The emergence of professional networking sites, such as LinkedIn, has made networking much easier, so much so that some job sites have direct links to social networking pages. These sites are used by millions of professionals and, used effectively, they can provide a powerful tool in your job search arsenal.

Basic accounts are often free and allow you to connect with other people in your profession, along with the people they know and so on. There are usually groups covering your particular job or area of interest where you can join discussions and pick up market intelligence.

Along with getting news about companies and the state of the job market, you can catch up with colleagues and let the relevant people know you are looking for work. Be aware, though, that an online social networking site is a public space. Nothing is private once it is posted unless you deliberately put a filter on it.

Online safety and protecting your privacy

Always use common sense and caution on the internet. Giving complete strangers confidential information means that, in the wrong hands, it could lead to difficult situations or even be quite damaging. Unfortunately, there are programs that crawl the internet seeking out personal information and, by posting your CV, you become vulnerable to them.

- Use reputable sites and keep a record of which ones you register with. If you are contacted by any organisations you don't recognise, ask them to confirm where they got your CV.

- No legitimate recruitment agency requires payment up front from the applicant, nor does it need your bank details.

- Take care with personal information such as your Social Security number and date of birth as this type of information can be used by identity thieves. Use secure pages.

- If you're checking a company, don't just click on the links it has provided; go to its website from an independent, outside source.

- Suspect any offer that's too good to be true, such as a highly paid job that requires no experience. Double-check before submitting any personal information. Try putting the company name and 'scam' into a search engine to see if anything comes up. You're probably not the first or the only person they've contacted.

- Protect your privacy by creating a user name and password for job search and career networking sites that are different from your private and work ones.

- Control unwanted e-mail – spam – by setting up a separate, dedicated e-mail address for your job search.

Any questions?

How do I change my CV into a plain-text one?

Copy your formatted CV (eg laid out with bullet points, heading in bold print, etc) into a new file. Convert what you see into plain text: take out all the bullet points, bold headings, underlining and italics and anywhere you've used 'tab' to indent. Change the font to a basic one such as Courier 12 point, which should translate into all e-mail systems.

Now reformat it so that it still looks reasonable. Make full use of spaces, capitals, asterisks, etc to achieve a reasonably presentable CV. Don't use any character that doesn't appear on your keyboard, and don't use the word-wrap feature; use 'enter' to create line breaks.

Save the file as a text-only document (eg mycv.txt). If you want to see how well it performs, open the file in Notepad (Windows's text editor) instead of Word and make any further necessary adjustments.

Chapter Six
Problems, problems

Overcoming problems is often a matter of emphasising some sections of your CV and playing down others. This chapter looks at how this applies to 20 of the most common problems in CV writing.

1. My CV would fill four pages, at least

The things you have done recently are more important to a prospective employer than things you did years ago. Highlight the skills that are most relevant to the job you are applying for. Detail your recent experience and summarise everything else.

Example

Career profile

(Give a brief career summary)
A skilled engineer with over 20 years' manufacturing experience in the engineering and furniture industries, including 10 years at senior management level. Currently developing a competitively driven organisation demanding high standards of performance.

Key skills

(Choose the most relevant ones)

- Operations and manufacturing management
- Logistics management using current tools and techniques

- Staff management: development and management of change strategy
- Financial management control, budget preparation
- Project management

Career history

(Go into detail about your current job...)
Pitman Ltd, Limpsfield
2007 to present
Operations Manager
Responsible for factories and staff within Operations Group

- Reorganised profile business and set up Logistics Support Centre, reducing operating costs by £150k
- Coordinated and managed activities in five factories and Logistics Support Centre, ensured effective running of operations supplying products to customers
- Formulated and implemented change programme in three factories to bring them level with rest of group
- Improved industrial relations, restoring management leadership with help of Partnership Agreement
- Increased financial performance of group by £300k overall
- Promoted to present position from Factory Manager 2009

Vollens Engineering, Stoke
2000 to 2007
Industrial Engineer
(... and briefly summarise earlier, less relevant ones)
Industrial engineering services at factory and divisional level. Provided production engineering service with particular emphasis on product costing, value engineering, pre-production engineering and methods improvement.

2. I've just left school/college/ university – what do I put in my CV?

This topic is covered fully in Chapter 7.

3. My work history isn't straightforward

If you have a wide range of skills, select those that are the most appropriate to the job you are applying for. Summarise the main themes of your career history in the Profile at the top of your CV and pick appropriate examples to illustrate your Key strengths. Organise the skills and experience you have acquired into groupings under appropriate headings, so that the full range of your skills is covered.

Example

CAREER PROFILE

(Emphasise any common threads or themes in your career that are relevant to the job you're applying for)
Sales and management professional with eight years' experience of customer-focused business including retail, telesales, commercial and face-to-face selling as well as business and staff management.
(What do all the jobs have in common? In this case, they're all customer focused.)

KEY SKILLS

Sales

- Maintaining and servicing existing accounts while developing new territory
- Liaising with distribution department to ensure efficient service to customers
- Developing new sales drive offering extended range of products to existing customers
- Producing quarterly analysis of sales by product and customer for head office records

Business management
Managing businesses, including a busy town centre café, requiring a range of skills, including:

- Purchasing stock
- Establishing pricing structures
- Marketing and promotion
- Bookkeeping
- Managing staff

CAREER HISTORY

(If your work history is confusing, summarise it briefly)

2009–present	Sales Representative	Bullseye Windows, Deanleigh
2007–2009	Manager	Corner's Cafe, Penbury
2003–2007	Manager	Dilly's Gifts, Fosbury
2001–2003	Sales Assistant	Dean Catering, Deansgate
2001	Telesales	Homer Ltd, Penbury, Representative
1997–2001	Cellarman and foodstoreman	Foss Hotel, Fosbury

4. I'm doing more than one job

This situation is becoming more common as people adapt to different career structures. You may be doing two part-time jobs instead of one full-time one, or you may be self-employed and also doing a part-time job, or a 'portfolio' worker, or a full-timer working on freelance contracts in your own time.

As shown in Problem 3 above, summarise the main theme of your career in a Profile, and organise your range of skills and experience under separate headings. When you come to your Career history, group your jobs together under the relevant date.

Example

Career history

2009 to present
Video Maker
Community Production Facility

- Planned, produced and directed seven 30–60 minute videos for The Parenting Initiative
- Decided with featured experts content and presentation of video
- Planned lighting, camera angles, camera shots
- Designed, produced and directed two independent video shorts

Radio Producer and Presenter
Valley Radio

- Researched, planned and presented weekly community arts slot on local radio
- Delivered reports
- Selected, approached and interviewed guests

Video Trainer/Facilitator
Kids TV, Community Youth Group

- Assisted youth group making youth and community videos
- Trained them in use of video equipment and basics of production and editing
- Coordinated sound, content and storyline

5. I've had a lot of jobs

Condense your employment record, focusing attention on the skills you have achieved through your experience, and only giving details of your most recent and most relevant positions. Jobs held more than 10 or 15 years ago can often be lumped together as 'various'.

Example

Employment record

2007–present   Logistica Ltd, Gwent
Production Manager

1999–2007   Owen Pearson, Gwent
Factory Manager
Industrial Engineer (promoted 2002)

1993–1999   Various
Engineering and supervisory

6. I'm changing careers

Use the Career profile at the head of your CV to make your new direction clear. Pick out your skills, qualities and achievements that are most appropriate to your new career and emphasise these, and give relevant examples in your Key strengths.

Example

CAREER PROFILE

Qualified counsellor with experience of working with young people under demanding conditions, looking to use and expand existing skills in a challenging and worthwhile situation where there is an opportunity for further development.

KEY QUALIFICATIONS

Certificate of Counselling Practice (AEB)
Certificate of Counselling Theory (AEB)

CAREER HISTORY

Volunteer Counsellor
Safe As Houses
2008 to present
Counselled young people with a variety of problems centring on homelessness. Managed a heavy caseload, giving advice and information on housing and benefit entitlements where appropriate, and participated in supervision and support meetings. Attended residential course on Means-tested Benefits by the Welfare Rights Unit.

Sales Receptionist
SAR TV & Video Rentals
2007 to 2011
Demonstrated, sold and arranged rentals of TVs and videos, handled cash and security, stock control, telephone enquiries and customer accounts.

7. My relevant experience is in voluntary/unpaid work

Voluntary positions are acceptable as part of your career history; see the example in Problem 6, above. The skills and experience you have gained from the job are as important as those gained from paid employment. Include them.

8. I haven't got much experience for the job I want to do

Make the most of what you can offer. Look at your qualifications, training, current experience – including both paid and unpaid work – and personal qualities. Make full use of the Key skills section, along with a Key achievement or Key experience section, whichever seems appropriate, to highlight everything that matches the job you want. Don't leave potential employers to dig out these important details from your CV for themselves.

If lack of experience is a serious handicap, consider 'alternative' ways of getting it, such as volunteering, an unpaid work-experience placement, temporary or part-time work, short-term contracts, or even taking a step down the career ladder in order to work your way up to a new position.

9. Most of the jobs I've done have been very much the same

Concentrate on your key skills and achievements and simply summarise your actual career history.

Example

Career profile

A smart, efficient sales consultant and confident in-store demonstrator, experienced in a number of sales environments including TV and video, white goods and home furnishings.

Key skills

- Customer care
- Cash handling and security
- Stock control, including operating computerised stock control system
- Financial administration, including credit agreements, customer accounts, credit/debit notes, and bank reconciliations
- Clerical administration, including sales reports and customer correspondence

Key achievements

- Organised and managed Sandlands stand at this year's Home Electric Exhibition
- Used computerised stock control system to track and analyse stock movement between five branches
- Organised daily bank deposits of cash and credit card takings
- Member of team winning 'Contact '09' award

Employment record

2009–present   Sandlands Sales and Marketing
Sales Demonstrator

2006–2009   TV Ten TV & Video Rentals
Sales Consultant

2004–2006   Whittaker Furnishings
Sales Consultant

10. I know I'm right for the job, but how can I get that across?

When you find a job that you know is just what you're looking for, take the time and trouble to prepare a CV specifically tailored for that vacancy, using the skills and qualities listed in the job advertisement or job description. Carefully match your own qualifications and experience to the employer's needs.

Chapter 3 has lots more information about how to customise your CV to make sure you get the message across clearly.

11. I'm over-qualified for the job I want

Emphasise the relevant *practical* skills and experience that you have for the job. Focus attention on your Key strengths and Key skills sections, and choose the skills that fit the job you are applying for. 'Excess' qualifications can be discreetly mentioned in the education section. Highlight, instead, any relevant on-the-job training you have had.

12. I don't have many qualifications

Concentrate on what you do have. Emphasise your practical skills and experience; these are often more valuable to an employer than theoretical knowledge anyway.

If your lack of qualifications is a serious handicap, consider applying for further training. This can often be undertaken in the workplace without the need to go back into full-time education. You may also find that your existing experience can be counted towards a qualification.

Example

Key skills

Customer care

- Receive and seat customers
- Take orders from customers and liaise with the kitchen
- Handle customer enquiries and complaints efficiently

Service

- Provide both à la carte and table d'hôte style service
- Perform silver service and French style food service
- Set tables for meals of up to eight courses
- Serve wine and other beverages
- Clear tables systematically

Key achievements

- Provided silver service at city centre four-star hotel, serving up to 600 people daily at breakfast, lunch and dinner
- Performed waitress service and bar service at major functions
- Served all types and levels of customers efficiently, pleasantly and courteously

13. I'm over 50

Make sure your CV clearly states your experience and successful track record – these things tend to come only with maturity – and stringently edit your early career history.

This subject is covered more fully in Chapter 9.

14. I'm under 25

You may appear to be lacking experience. Emphasise any experience you do have, and highlight any skills you may have from school or college, even if you haven't had the opportunity to use them in a work setting.

This subject is covered more fully in Chapter 7.

15. I'm returning to work after bringing up children

Stress your capabilities, qualities and experience. Highlight any skills and experience you have gained in voluntary positions in the home, school, or in the community, as well as any training or re-training you may be doing in preparation for your return to work.

This subject is covered more fully in Chapter 8.

16. I'm applying for two different types of jobs

If you're applying for different jobs requiring different attributes, you will need to have two different CVs, each with a different emphasis.

The following two CVs have been prepared for the same person, the first concentrating on training experience and the second concentrating on sales experience:

Guy Owen
33 Holly Court
Prince's Road
Leeds LS5 2AS

Telephone: 0000 000 0000
E-mail: gowen@anyisp.uk

Career profile

A skilled trainer with over 12 years' experience in training and allied fields. Currently undertaking a wide range of consultative training initiatives in both the private and public sector. Also responsible for the effective coordination of professional services within the company.

Key strengths

The ability to analyse individual training needs: consistently achieved and exceeded training targets by working with trainees as individuals and assessing their specific needs rather than delivering a 'one-size-fits-all' package.

Excellent presentation and communication skills: awarded the Technical Training prize two years running in recognition of my presentation and communication skills.

Training experience

- Successfully trained and licensed a sales force of 50 within three months
- Designed and implemented a new monitoring and assessment system
- Established management training for Branch Sales Managers
- Consistently achieved sales training targets
- Devised and wrote training manuals
- Awarded Technical Training Prize 2009 and 2010

Career summary

2008–present	Training Consultant	ICS Training
2005–2008	Area Sales Manager	Ellenbach Assurance
2001–2005	Head of Sales Training	Mutual Assurance Financiers
1996–2001	Sales Manager	Bradford-Bond Brokerage
1993–1996	Sales Associate	Crown Corporate Investments

Education and training

2001	ASA Associates	Certificate in Training
1991–1993	South Bradley College	HNC Business Studies

Member of the Life Assurance Association

Personal

Date of birth: 17 November 1973

Full, clean UK driving licence

References available on request

Guy Owen
33 Holly Court
Prince's Road
Leeds LS5 2AS

Telephone: 0000 000 0000
E-mail: gowen@anyisp.uk

Career profile

A Senior Sales Executive with a background in sales management, specific experience of business-to-business negotiations and a proven track record in business systems, office supplies and business machines.

Key strengths

A solid background in sales: 15 years' experience of sales and sales training up to Area Sales Manager level and a personal track record in direct selling with a client base exceeding 600 in five years.

Solution selling/consultative approach: achieved an increase of 20 per cent annual profit through rigorously using a consultative approach with clients, and trained sales staff how to achieve the same results.

Sales experience

- Personal sales track record in direct selling with a client base exceeding 600 in five years
- Increased sales by 20 per cent over preceding year's totals
- Formulated major policy decisions on all stages of sales activities
- Responsible for new product launches
- Achieved competitive advantage through thorough knowledge of the market
- Successfully set up sales training programme

Career summary

2008–present	Training Consultant	ICS Training
2005–2008	Area Sales Manager	Ellenbach Assurance
2001–2005	Head of Sales Training	Mutual Assurance Financiers
1996–2001	Sales Manager	Bradford-Bond Brokerage
1993–1996	Sales Associate	Crown Corporate Investments

Education and training

1991–1993	South Bradley College	HNC Business Studies
2001	ASA Associates	Certificate in Training

Member of the Life Assurance Association

Personal

Date of birth: 17 November 1973

Full, clean UK driving licence

References available on request

17. I've been unemployed for over a year

As with many of the problems above, the answer is to emphasise your positive points and give these the major share of your CV, and to cover only briefly those areas where you may be weaker.

Include the skills you have learnt through voluntary work or further training during your period of unemployment. In the example below, the job as Finance Administrator was a full-time voluntary position, but attention isn't drawn to this fact.

Example

KEY SKILLS

Management

- Managing and motivating five full-time and up to 20 part-time staff in three branches
- Maximising savings, mortgage sales, and introducing customer services including mortgage debt counselling
- Exceeding targets set for insurance, savings and mortgage lending sales
- Representing Mutual Assurance Group on committee of local Chamber of Commerce

Financial administration

- Running purchase order system and budget control
- Preparing month-end accounts and monthly business reports
- Compiling Management Information Reports and preparing claims for Government Agencies
- Organising and administering payment of office and staff expenses

Information technology
Proficient in using both spreadsheet and word-processing applications:

- Word
- Excel
- Access
- Outlook
- PowerPoint

CAREER SUMMARY

Currently	Information Technology NVQ level 3	Data Training
2008–2010	Finance Administrator	Cosmopolitan Trust
2004–2008	Group Branch Manager	Mutual Assurance Group
1996–2004	Travel Agency Manager	Bond Travel

18. I have two quite different areas of experience

This is similar to Problem 16. Consider preparing two different CVs, each highlighting one of your two main areas of experience, and using them as appropriate, depending on the type of job you're applying for.

19. My last job was actually a bit of a step backwards (or sideways)

With so many organisations changing their structure and even cutting out whole layers of management, this is true for many people these days.

Don't draw attention to it. Put your abilities and achievements in a separate, major, section and just summarise the rest of your employment details.

Example

Key skills

- Providing a Help Desk for software and hardware queries
- Using VMS and RSX operating systems to recover lost data files
- Analysing system performance, identifying problems and establishing their probable origin before taking appropriate action
- Error logging for both software and hardware

- Installation and implementation of communications equipment using X21, KILOSTREAM and MERCURY links
- Daily backup of data records and transfer of these records to off-site storage
- General maintenance of hardware and data wiring

Career summary

2005–present	Programmer	Sunstream Industries
2001–2005	System Controller	Trust Insurance
1997–2001	Senior System Analyst	Ringwood Assurance
1992–1997	Programmer, data storage and retrieval	Various

20. I've only ever had one job

Make sure you cover the full range of skills you've used in that job, and include any experience gained from outside interests or voluntary work that will usefully expand your abilities.

Example

Career profile

A well-organised, reliable secretary and receptionist with extensive knowledge of good office practice including word processing, desktop publishing, electronic mail systems, spreadsheets and databases.

Key skills

Secretarial

- RSA III Typewriting – current speed 70 wpm
- RSA II Audio-typing – current speed 70 wpm
- RSA II Shorthand – current speed 120 wpm
- Typing all correspondence and reports
- Preparing spreadsheets and maintaining databases
- Arranging, coordinating and minuting all departmental meetings

Reception

- Operating 20-line switchboard
- Directing all incoming calls, and dealing initially with all queries
- Administering incoming and outgoing mail
- Handling all enquiries at reception, including visitors and deliveries

Career history

Link Holdings Ltd
2007 to present
Receptionist, Secretary to Marketing Department

Chapter Seven
Starting out

Whether you're leaving school, college or university, what do you put in your CV when you're just starting out?

Personal statement

Without a career history to tell them what sort of interests and aptitudes you have, potential employers can form a clearer picture of you from a well thought-out personal statement.

It can be quite useful to know what you feel your positive qualities are, what you see as your main strengths at this early stage, and also an idea of the direction you hope your career will take.

Key strengths

This is your best opportunity to demonstrate your suitability for the job. However and wherever you achieved them, if you have skills that match the job requirements, make sure you highlight them.

Qualifications

At this stage in your career, Education and training are probably going to be one of the important sections, so cover them fully – especially if you have been doing a college or university course closely related to the sort of work that you want to do.

Achievements

Highlight any special duties or responsibilities you have undertaken at school or college.

Include anything that rounds out the picture of you as a responsible and dependable individual with experience of more than just the classroom or lecture hall. Convince your future employer that you have qualities that will be useful to them in the workplace.

Work experience

A prospective employer will be interested in any work experience you've had. It doesn't matter if your experience is different from the sort of work you are applying for; it will still demonstrate that you are familiar with a working environment. You can show that you appreciate the importance of punctuality, following instructions, being responsible, etc.

Your experience needn't necessarily be in paid employment. Include any voluntary work that you may have done, as well as internships, work placements or work experience courses, especially if they are relevant to the sort of work that you wish to do.

For more ideas about the sort of qualities employers value, see the section on *Desirable qualities* in Chapter 16.

Examples of school and college leavers' CVs appear on the following pages. Keep in mind that the Key strengths section of each CV was based specifically on the 'The successful candidate will have…' statement in the job ad it was written for and will therefore change with each new application.

The first example – Pamela Heart's – shows how even a rather sparse CV can be customised to give much more information. The ad it was written in reply to is included so that you can see exactly how she uses her Key strengths section to address the employer's stated needs.

Pamela Heart – before and after CVs for a school leaver without work experience, but with some voluntary work experience.

Angela Walker – school leaver with relevant skills and experience.

Richard Quinlan – school leaver with relevant work experience.

Anthony Dickens – college leaver with some relevant work experience.

Linda Darin – college leaver with some work experience.

Kevin Clarke – graduate with excellent work experience.

Yolande Eden – university graduate with some work experience.

Pamela Heart's 'before' CV

Pamela Heart
87 First Road
Impney
Hereford HE15 6TD

Tel: 00000 000000
e-mail: princess@partyparty.co.uk

Education

2004–2011 Heath House King's School
GCSEs:
    French B
    History C
    Maths C
    General Science C
    English Language D
A levels:
    French C
    History C

Work experience

2011 – Volunteer sheltered housing aid visitor
2010 and 2011 – Volunteer coach for holiday play scheme

Interests

Tennis and badminton, athletics, socialising and meeting new people

Date of birth: 20 April 1993

A very sparse CV with little for an employer to get their teeth into. But even this CV can be improved. This is the job ad that Pamela replied to:

Customer Care Team

Hours: Monday to Friday 0900–1700
Salary: £_____ pa

Working in our Customer Enquiries Office, you will be computer literate and have good communication skills. An articulate, friendly, helpful manner would be an advantage.

This position would suit a school leaver. Full training will be given, and there are many opportunities for advancement within the company.

Please contact _____.

Pamela knew she had the skills and personal qualities needed to do the job and customised her CV so that the employer knew it too.

Pamela Heart's 'after' CV

Pamela Heart
87 First Road
Impney
Hereford HE15 6TD

Tel: 00000 000000
e-mail: psheart@anyisp.co.uk

Personal profile

A friendly, outgoing person. Reliable, conscientious and happy to work both as part of a team and on own initiative.

Key strengths

Good communication skills and a helpful manner: voluntary work with both elderly people and younger children has developed a good range of communication skills as well as the ability to help and support others conscientiously and diplomatically.

IT skills: full PC literacy including spreadsheets, e-mail, the internet and word processing

Achievements

- Represented the school in Athletics and Cross-Country Running
- Participated in City Marathon 2011
- Secretary of Under-18 Squash and Racquet team
- Elected House Captain

Education

2004–2011 Heath House King's School
A levels:
French C; History C
Computer skills
Microsoft XP including:
    Word
    Access
    Excel
GCSEs:
French B; History C; Maths C; General Science C; English Language D

Work experience

2010 – Working with elderly people: regularly visited four residents of local sheltered housing to help with shopping and everyday household tasks.

2010 and 2011 – Holiday play scheme: coached under-11s in squash, badminton and tennis in groups of four or five during summer and Easter holidays.

Personal details

Date of birth: 20 April 1993
Non-smoker

Pamela's new CV is not only more informative generally but also tells the employer exactly what they want to know. Note the change of e-mail address, by the way.

Richard Quinlan
9 Barge's Brook Lane
Upper Tindle
Warwickshire WR3 6VN

Tel: 0000 0000000

PERSONAL PROFILE

School leaver with workplace experience, a good eye for detail and the ability to work well both independently and as part of a team. With a particular interest in retail work, either sales or marketing.

KEY STRENGTHS

Previous retail experience: part-time and holiday experience at a local newsagent and a soft-furnishings shop has taught me the value of punctuality and of following instructions accurately, and also developed confidence in my ability to relate to customers and to handle everyday problems appropriately.

Enthusiastic, ambitious and dedicated to customer service: while at Drum House Furnishings, I was trained to listen to customers, identify their requirements and recommend products that would best suit their needs, a role that I greatly enjoyed and wish to develop further.

EDUCATION

2006–2011 City Park School
GCSEs:
General Science B; English language A; Maths C; German B; History B

EMPLOYMENT

Kay News newsagents
2009 – present
Newspaper Distributor

- Sorted deliveries
- Delivered newspapers and magazines reliably
- Handled enquiries and complaints
- Collected cash

Drum House Furnishings
Summer 2011
Sales and Storeroom Assistant

- Served and assisted customers
- Maintained displays
- Took details of customer orders
- Prepared orders for distribution office

PERSONAL DETAILS

Date of birth: 1 February 1995
Health: Non-smoker
Interests: Acting and stage management. I belong to the local amateur
                dramatics club and am secretary to the Drama Youth Group.
References: Available on request

Angela Walker
31 Pollard Way
Marsh Cross
Cambridge CM14 2KL
Tel: 0000 0000000
e-mail: awalker@anyisp.com

PERSONAL PROFILE

A highly motivated school leaver with experience of office work. Punctual, reliable and willing to learn, with a good basic education and a strong aptitude for organisation and administration.

KEY STRENGTHS

Experience of office work: I have been an after-school voluntary assistant in the school office for the past year, supporting the school secretary and helping with all aspects of administration. My summer work experience was also as an office assistant with a firm of estate agents, carrying out routine office procedures.

Computer literate: trained in Microsoft Office with experience of using Word and Excel.

KEY SKILLS

- Keyboard skills – 40 wpm
- Preparing and writing routine correspondence
- Organising and carrying out routine administrative work
  - maintaining records
  - dealing with incoming telephone calls
  - dealing with incoming mail

WORK EXPERIENCE

Ashbourn & Sedley, Summer 2010
Office Assistant

Marsh Cross School Administration Department, 2010–2011
Administrative Assistant (part-time/voluntary)

EDUCATION

2004–2011 Marsh Cross School
GCSEs:
  English language
  English literature
  Maths
  French
  History
  Economics

Introduction to Computer Literacy
RSA Stage I Keyboard Skills
RSA Stage I Office Skills

PERSONAL DETAILS

Date of birth: 30 March 1993

Interests: Riding and pony-trekking, reading and cinema

References available on request

Anthony Dickens
7 Yelland Avenue
Port Nearsby
Pickering PS12 7HG
Tel: 0000 0000000
e-mail: adickens@anyisp.com

Personal profile

College graduate with BTEC in Business and Finance and work experience in a banking environment.

Key strengths

Self-motivated and hard-working: have arranged all work experience placements on my own initiative and fulfilled all requirements to the highest satisfaction of each employer. Consistently in top 5 per cent of class for college course.

An understanding of the financial environment: have had work experience at three different banks with the opportunity to observe a comprehensive range of financial procedures.

Education and training

2010 to 2011, Thorford College: **BTEC National Diploma in Business and Finance, Year 2**
    Administration systems
    Business environment
    Human resources
    Financial planning and control
    Elements of investment
    Innovation and change
    Business statistics
    Personnel, policies and procedures
    Insurance two

2009 to 2010, Thorford College: **BTEC National Diploma in Business and Finance, Year 1**
  Principles and practice of insurance
  Elements of banking
  Accounting procedures
  Business Information Technology
  Financial resources
  Physical resources
  Marketing process

2008 to 2009, Eastville College of Further Education: **BTEC First Diploma in Business and Finance**
  Insurance proficiency one
  Production
  Business Information Technology
  Administrative support
  People in business
  Business resources and procedures
  Administrative systems and procedures
  Business world

Work history

2010 to present:
  Bealsway, Corington
  Cashier and Kiosk Assistant
  Responsibilities: Handled large amounts of money; Customer care; Alcohol and cigarette legislation

Work experience

  National Associative Bank, Corington

  Lakeland Bank, Corington

  Mansfield Bank, Pickering

  Responsibilities: Carried out basic office procedures and clerical work, including filing and photocopying. Observed and assessed departmental procedures including:
  – Foreign exchange
  – Mortgage and lending
  – Pensions
  – High-risk accounts
  – Customer services
  – Processing room

Additional skills

Computer skills: Microsoft Office
Familiarity with Windows environment, and use of spreadsheets and databases.

Personal

Date of birth: 18 May 1991
Interests: I enjoy riding and swimming, and support my local football and basketball teams. I also enjoy listening to music.

References: Available on request

Linda Darin
34 Southernwood Drive
Hendy Hill
Edgerton
Surrey SR21 9AS

Tel. 00000 000000
e-mail: ldarin@anyisp.com

PERSONAL PROFILE

College graduate with sales and voluntary work experience looking for an entry-level opportunity in travel and tourism that will allow me to make use of my theoretical knowledge while acquiring practical skills.

KEY STRENGTHS

Good customer relations skills: my experience of working with the public in retail, fundraising and youth work has taught me the value of friendliness, open-mindedness and having a good sense of humour as well as how to communicate effectively at all levels.

Qualification in environmental, tourism or related subject area: I have recently completed a two-year BTEC National Diploma in Travel and Tourism.

Competent IT skills: trained and experienced in using Word, Excel and Outlook Express.

EMPLOYMENT

Hall Dean Markets, 2008–2009
Sales Assistant

- Served and assisted customers
- Handled cash
- Dealt with enquiries and complaints

Voluntary work experience

- Raised funds for CCRF (Childhood Cancer Relief Fund)
- Worked with children with learning difficulties

EDUCATION AND TRAINING

2009–2011 Edgerton College
BTEC National Diploma in Travel and Tourism
The course covered all aspects of travel and tourism, including:

- Worldwide travel geography
- Airport operations
- Resort representatives
- Finance
- Travel services

Language skills:

- Spanish
- German
- Italian
- French

Computer skills:

- Word
- Access

2003–2009 Edgerton School
GCSEs:
Five including Maths and English
Services to Business
Services to People

PERSONAL DETAILS

Date of birth:	19 July 1992
Driving licence:	Full, clean UK licence
Interests:	Member of: Edgerton hockey club, Edgerton athletics club, Southland athletics club, Affiliated to the BSJA (horse riding)

References: Available on request

Kevin Clarke
16 Whiteside Gardens
Kesdale
Lincs LN5 7TU
Tel: (0132) 0000000
e-mail: kclarke@unorth.ac.uk

Personal profile

Biological Sciences graduate with first-hand laboratory and administrative experience in an industrial environment and an understanding of the requirements of a commercial organisation. Quick to learn and used to adapting to high pressure and tight deadlines while remaining both good-humoured and accurate.

Work experience

Summer 2011
Dale Chemicals
Laboratory Assistant:

- Responsible for trials of chemical scrubbing techniques
- Administered trial process
- Analysed data and prepared reports accordingly

Summer 2010
Seabright Pharmaceuticals
General Assistant:

- Coordinated administration of full-scale drug trials
- Responsible for data collation requiring 100% accuracy
- Prepared interim reports
- Carried out administrative requirements of the department

Education

2008–2011, University of the North
 BSc (Hons) Biological Sciences – 2(ii)

2001–2008, Kesdale High School
 GCSEs: Seven GCSEs including Maths and English
 A levels: Maths, Chemistry, Biology

Computer literacy: Word, Access
Languages: Conversational French

Personal details

Date of birth	15 November 1990
Interests	Reading, swimming, music
References	Available on request

Yolande Eden
77 Terrence Place
Long Common
Cheshire CH15 8SX
Tel: (0000) 0000000
e-mail: yeden@wmu.ac.uk

Career objective:	A Computer Science graduate with a keen interest in applications and information systems, seeking a career where a background in problem solving would be an advantage.
Key strengths: A self-starter with a high level of initiative:	Devised and implemented design of final-year project, proposed it to West Midlands NHS and delivered new geographical database currently used by department.
Strong organisation and planning skills:	Planned and organised comprehensive programme for summer FutureFit project with a team of five, giving local schools hands-on coaching and demonstrations of how technology can improve sports performance.
Fast learner who thrives in a rapidly changing environment:	Learned to use GI Systems in three weeks in order to undertake final-year project. My interest in robotics and AI attests to my interest in leading-edge, rapidly changing technology.

Education:

2008–2011: **BSc Computer Science,** West Midlands University

Year 3:

Robotics:	**Database Theory:**
concepts	structure
VAL	storage
3-D modelling of	design
components	**Formal Logic:**
assembly	trinary
matrices	fuzzy
Graphics:	temporal
2-D and 3-D	**Artificial Intelligence:**
projection	PopII
transformation matrices	expert systems
Communications:	Prolog
network theory	theory of neural nets
protocols	
hardware	

Final-Year Project:

The Use of Geographical Information Systems. The project was to write a geographical database which, using a GIS package, could plot NHS patient data for the West Midlands. Project included use of OS map data. Package used: Arc-Info under X-Windows on a DEC workstation.

Year 2:

Computer Science:	**Maths:**
database design with	transformation
SSADM	matrices with
Ad programming	coordinate systems
micro-electronics	multiple differentiation
formal logic	integration
software design methods	

Year 1:

Computer Science:	**Maths:**
software management	graphs and matrices
programming	complex equations
methodologies	differential equations
micro-electronics	integration with
programming in Ada	trigonometric functions

Key skills:

Programming languages:

Ada	SML
Pascal	C
Popll	Modula 2
Prolog	Clipper 5
VAL	ArcInfo

Environments:

Sunview	Apple Mac
X-Windows	UNIX
MS-Windows	MSDOS

Work experience:

Summer 2010: **Tripp Electronics**, Littledean
Administrative Assistant

Summer 2009: **Torrington Newcombe**, Olstead
Clerical Assistant

Summer 2008: **Tripp Electronics**, Littledean
Clerk

Personal:

Date of birth: 19 January 1986

Full, clean UK driving licence

Interests: I am an active member of the University Irish Folk Club and enjoy
music, listening and performing, and dancing. I also enjoy cycling and
swimming.

Chapter Eight
Starting again

At some time in your life, you may find yourself re-entering the job market after a break. This can be for a number of reasons: bringing up a family, taking time out for travel or voluntary work, or redundancy or unemployment.

Don't apologise for your career break. Gaps in employment, for whatever reason, are a fact of life and should be handled positively and assertively.

Emphasise your relevant experience and concentrate on your skills and qualities. Draw attention to what you have done, rather than what you haven't.

Career profile

You may be returning to a different type of job from the one that you used to do. If so, make use of the Career profile at the top of the page to connect the three parts of your working life: your previous employment, your experience during the break, and your future direction.

Key strengths

This is your most obvious opportunity to demonstrate that you have the key skills and experience needed for the job, however and wherever you achieved them. Make sure you are highlighting an excellent match.

Key skills

Highlight your key skills, achievements or qualifications. Include any gained through voluntary or part-time work during your career break. Include, too, qualifications and skills gained through education or training, and mention any ways in which you have kept abreast of developments in your trade or profession.

You might like to add positive ways in which you have changed: increased maturity, for example, or more responsibility, confidence, understanding, new skills, insight, etc.

Career history

What have you done during your break?

Depending on how long you have been out of employment, things may have changed a lot since you last worked. Employers worry about returners being out of date with what's happening in the industry. They may wonder if you will be willing to adapt to new ways of doing things.

Point out how you have kept up your skills, and mention anything that you have done to improve or update them. Any training you have done during this time will be a useful indicator of your interest and motivation. It's a good idea, in any case, to go back to the workplace better qualified than when you left it.

Include all the work experience you have had during your career break, including voluntary work, part-time work, special responsibilities and duties, etc. Even if it was unpaid, an employer will still be interested in what you have done recently.

Examples of workplace returners' CVs appear on the following pages. Keep in mind that the Key strengths section of each CV was based specifically on the 'The successful candidate will have...' statement in the job ad it was written for and will therefore change with each new application.

The first example – Joy Perris – shows how her CV was extensively improved and customised to give much more information. The ad it was written in reply to is also shown so that you can see exactly how she uses her Key strengths section to highlight her excellent match to the employer's stated needs.

Joy Perris – before and after CVs for someone returning after childcare with updated training.

Janet Sandiman – returning after childcare, looking for a career change after training.

Ananda Vires – returning after childcare, voluntary work experience.

Daniel Guys – returning to full-time work after extensive travelling.

Edward Kingsman – returning after redundancy with further training and related voluntary work.

Diane Walker – returning after redundancy with updated training.

Joy Perris's 'before' CV

CURICULUM VITAE

SURNAME: **PERRIS**
FORENAMES: **JOY HELEN MARY**
DATE OF BIRTH: **12/5/79**
ADDRESS: 27 KINGSCOTE PLACE, LIMPNEY, SURREY SR1 2AA
TELEPHONE: 00000 000000

EDUCATION
September 2010 – Present
Limpney Training Centre: CLAIT and Clerical/Supervisory Skills Course

October 1998 – June 2000
South London College: German GCSE (Evening Class), Pass

September 1990 – July 1995
Porton Comprehensive: obtained GCSE passes in English Language, English Literature, Needlework, Biology, History, Maths

EMPLOYMENT HISTORY
2008–present – childcare

2004–2008 – Mutual Assurance Association
General Office Supervisor
Responsible for collation and administration of documents and records; the organisation of data within the department; dealing with queries to the department.

1997–2004 – Clipper Retail
Shop Assistant, rising to Duty Manager
Supervised staff and attended to customers in busy city-centre store. Responsible for daily administration of section including stock control, cashing up, section turnover and customer complaints.

1995–1997 – Danube Imports Ltd
Clerical Assistant

HOBBIES AND INTERESTS
I enjoy music, dancing and aerobics, and was a keen member of the parent governors' committee.

Joy thought her CV was a bit too basic, so when she decided to reply to the following job ad, she revised her CV extensively and tailored it to draw attention to her suitability for the position.

Administration Supervisor

Owing to expansion, an Administration Supervisor vacancy has arisen in our Data Management department. The successful candidate will be responsible for two Data Support staff and directly involved in maintaining, updating and creating data files, ensuring that our clients get the best service possible, as well as all other aspects of administration. Accuracy and attention to detail are crucial, and applicants must possess good communication skills with the ability to work under pressure during peak periods. Excellent IT skills in general and knowledge of Word and Excel in particular are essential. Experience of high-volume data handling preferred, but full training will be given.

Joy Perris's 'after' CV

JOY PERRIS
27 Kingscote Place
Limpney, Surrey SR1 2AA

Tel: 00000 000000

Career profile

Office Supervisor with four years' experience of organising data and records, and the tried and tested ability to maintain a consistently high standard of work and attention to detail under pressure and to motivate staff to do the same. Now looking for a challenging work environment where recently updated and enhanced computer skills can be put to good use ensuring the efficient working of a busy and demanding department.

Key strengths

Excellent IT skills: recently completed an advanced CLAIT course with a mark of 94%, having used computer skills extensively in a position of office supervisor.

Supervisory skills: successfully completed NVQ level 3 in Administration and Supervision and have been responsible for staff both as an office supervisor and as a retail duty manager.

Accuracy and attention to detail: retrieved and administered a large volume of documents and records for a busy insurance company to the highest degree of satisfaction of both internal clients and the Department Manager.

Client focused with good communication skills: used to dealing with sometimes complex interdepartmental queries courteously and efficiently as well as having been trained in customer focus in a retail environment.

Key skills

- Supervising staff
- Implementing procedures accurately
- Prioritising workload
- Computer skills – Microsoft Office Word, Excel, PowerPoint, Outlook

Career history

2010 – present: Limpney Training Centre
CLAIT advanced course to update and extend IT and office management skills

NVQ level 3 Clerical Skills Course; Administration and Supervision Course undertaken as part of return to work strategy following full-time childcare responsibilities

2004–2008: Mutual Assurance Association
Office Supervisor
Responsible for collation and administration of documents and records; the organisation of data within the department; and dealing with queries to the department.

- Successfully trained a total of four administrative assistants
- Developed new procedures as the department grew, maintaining the highest standards of efficiency and accuracy
- Reorganised the query process to provide a more user-friendly format
- Established comprehensive basic procedures manual for staff training purposes

1997–2004: Clipper Retail Stores
Duty Manager
Supervised a total of seven staff and attended to customers in busy city-centre store. Responsible for daily administration of section including stock control, cashing up, section turnover and customer complaints.

- Maintained store within top 5% turnover
- Reduced shoplifting and petty pilfering by 20% by slightly altering section layout
- Reviewed sales training with regard to administering the Lottery, leading to a substantial reduction in customer complaints
- Promoted from Retail Assistant in 2000

1995–1997: Danube Imports Ltd
Clerical Assistant
Dealt with office administration including bookkeeping and invoicing.

Education

Porton Comprehensive – 6 GCSE passes, including English and Maths
South London College – GCSE pass in German
Limpney Training Centre – CLAIT and NVQ3 Clerical, Administration and Supervisory Skills

Personal details

Date of birth – 12 May 1979
Health – Non-smoker
Driving – Full, clean UK licence
Proficient German speaker
Interests – Music, dancing, aerobics. Served as a Parent Governor on primary school Governing Body; involved in decisions on budgets, curriculum and other management issues.

JANET SANDIMAN
14 Eastover Common, Oxhill
Avon AV20 4CP
Tel: 0000 0000000
e-mail: jmnsandiman@anyisp.com

CAREER OBJECTIVE

A mature and responsible individual with counselling skills and broad experience of nursing and caring for others, now looking for the opportunity to work with clients and assist them to explore their concerns, focus on underlying issues, and consider options towards setting and achieving goals.

KEY STRENGTHS

Experience of building a long-term relationship with clients: AEB/CAC training is practical-skills based and includes experience of building client relationships both short (brief therapy) and long term.

Ability to relate to people of different backgrounds: as a nurse, required to deal tactfully, sympathetically and effectively with people of all ages and backgrounds and help them to feel as comfortable as possible in a strange and often intimidating environment.

KEY SKILLS

- Encouraging and motivating others
- Providing counselling support for trauma and bereavement
- Preparing others for, and supporting them through, life changes
- An understanding of women's health issues
- Computer literate

KEY QUALIFICATIONS

- State Enrolled Nurse
- Certificate of Counselling Theory AEB/CAC
- Certificate of Counselling Practice AEB/CAC
- Open Access vocational training in:
  - Post-trauma Stress and Critical Incident Debriefing
  - Primary Health Care Counselling
  - Managing Short-term Counselling Work within Primary Care
  - Women and Mental Health

CAREER HISTORY

2005 – present
Responsible for the full-time care of my two children, now at school, while also undergoing training as a counsellor.

2001–2005
Leigh House Hospital
State Enrolled Nurse
Responsible for medical and surgical patients:

- Prepared patients physically and mentally for surgery
- Provided patient care post-surgery
- Supported and counselled relatives of terminal patients
- Assisted on ward rounds
- Updated patient records
- Administered drugs
- Dealt with enquiries from patients and their families

1999–2001
Eastern Hospital
State Enrolled Nurse
Responsible for day-to-day working in out-patients department:

- Supported patients and provided patient care
- Assisted with routine procedures
- Dealt with enquiries from patients and their families
- Prepared working areas
- Compiled patient records

EDUCATION AND TRAINING

2006–2008 Westbrook College of Further Education
    Certificate of Counselling Theory AEB/CAC
    Certificate of Counselling Practice AEB/CAC

2007–2010 Oxhill Community College, Open Access vocational courses:
    Post-trauma Stress and Critical Incident Debriefing
    Primary Health Care Counselling
    Managing Short-term Counselling Work within Primary Care
    Women and Mental Health

1995–1997 Langport Hospital, Student Nurse for State Enrolled Nurse

1990–1995 St Lawrence School for Girls
    Six GCSEs, including Maths, English, Chemistry and Biology

PERSONAL DETAILS

Date of birth: 9 July 1981
Driving licence: Full, clean UK licence, own car
Interests: Computers, education, active member of the Oxhill community
    volunteers group
References: Available on request

Ananda Vires
2 Gorstan Mead, Matley
North Yorkshire NY19 7DC
Tel: 0000 0000000

CAREER PROFILE

A reliable, conscientious and efficient computer-literate administrator with good secretarial and organisational skills. Proficient at working both on own initiative and as part of a team.

KEY STRENGTHS

Efficient: as secretary of the Residents Association, required to turn around correspondence and reports in the shortest time possible and keep all interested parties informed and up to date. Responsible for planning meetings, ensuring venues are booked, members and guests notified, relevant paperwork available and any mishaps dealt with. Voted in as secretary three years running and given special vote of thanks for excellent work.

Reliable: have proved totally dependable as association secretary, as a working-party member, member of several committees and Tenants Forum representative, giving 100 per cent commitment to any role I take on.

Articulate: required to liaise with the Housing Office and to represent the Association at meetings of the Tenants Forum and at special interest groups.

KEY SKILLS

Secretarial, including word processing
    Word for Windows
    Excel
    Microsoft Outlook
Excellent telephone manner
Resourceful, reliable team member

CAREER HISTORY

Matley North End Residents Association
2007 – ongoing
Secretary
Organised and administered voluntary Tenants Association:

- Organised monthly meetings and annual general meetings
- Wrote, typed and circulated minutes
- Dealt with correspondence
- Liaised with Housing Office
- Drafted reports on specific issues as member of various working parties
- Represented Association at meetings of other organisations, the Tenants Forum and special interest groups

2003 – present
During this period I have also been caring for my children full-time.

Benn, Hodge and Keen
1998–2003
Secretary
Responsible for secretarial support to department:

- Typed reports and correspondence
- Organised appointments and arranged meetings
- Minuted all departmental meetings
- Responded to telephone enquiries and requests
- Coordinated department work schedule

Coburg & Partners
1993–1998
Secretary/clerk
Organised and carried out routine office administration, maintained records and files, dealt with incoming mail, prepared routine correspondence.

EDUCATION

Community Open College, 2010–2011
    Computer Literacy (CLAIT) Stages I & II
    Introduction to Information Technology
    RSA Stage I Office Skills
Holm Place School, 1986–1994
    GCSEs: Seven including Maths and English
    A levels: English Language, English Literature, French

PERSONAL DETAILS

Date of birth: 10 March 1975
Interests: Badminton, swimming
Car owner/driver with full, clean UK licence
References available on request

Daniel Guys
68 St John's Road
Adrington
East Sussex SX4 2JN
Tel: 0000 0000000

Career profile:

A graduate with first-rate language skills gained through both formal study and extensive travel, as well as teaching English as a Foreign Language in Europe, seeking a position that will allow me to use my experience and abilities to good effect in a forward-thinking, Europe-orientated organisation.

Key strengths:

Europe-focused, with knowledge of at least one European language: have lived and worked in France, Spain and Sweden, interacting with local and business communities. French and Spanish speaking.

Drive and initiative: devised and delivered property-focused Business English course for small businesses; devised suitable material for student language groups; self-funded all travel through finding work or sponsorship.

Key skills:

Languages
  Fluent written and spoken French: Conversational, Business, Literary
  Excellent Business and Conversational Spanish
Tuition
  Teaching Business English to Spanish business people in on-site training programmes
  Teaching Adult Education classes in France
  Teaching student groups in Swedish summer school
Other
  Computer literate, including word-processing packages and spreadsheets
  Experienced in meeting deadlines, dealing with clients, office procedures, and compiling records

Work experience:

Travelling in Africa, Asia and Europe, 2007–2011
Teacher of English as a Foreign Language
Responsible for teaching English to a variety of students:

- Delivered teaching programmes to several professional companies
- Taught Business English at all levels from students to company directors
- Devised and taught mixed-ability adult evening class
- Encouraged and motivated students
- Organised leisure activities for multilingual groups of students at residential summer school

Torrington Ellis Ltd, 2005–2007
Claims Supervisor
Initially employed as a graduate clerk/trainee, I was promoted to Claims Supervisor:

- Dealt with telephone enquiries and correspondence
- Processed claims
- Issued cheques
- Ensured deadlines were kept
- Prepared claims

Education:

South East College, 2008
RSA Certificate: Teaching English as a Foreign Language

University of East Midlands, 2002–2006
BA Hons 2:1, French Language and Literature

Fairchurch Secondary School, 1995–2002
GCSEs: Seven including Maths and English
A levels: English Literature, French, History

Personal details:

Date of birth: 10 August 1984
Interests: Foreign cinema, food and cookery, hill-walking
Health: Non-smoker
Prepared to relocate
References available on request

Edward Kingsman
The Firs, 8 Langport Road
Coveringham
Lincoln LN12 2JH

Tel: 0000 0000000
e-mail: ekingsman@anyisp.com

Career profile

A skilled engineer with both practical and managerial skills, gained through many years' experience of supervising staff including apprentices and trainees. An outgoing, down-to-earth person who enjoys being involved with whatever is going on, and has encountered and solved many problems with both machines and people.

Key skills

- Managing staff in a high-turnover production environment
- Providing a first-rate engineering service to internal and external customers
- Project management and budget preparation
- Training and motivating staff
- Computer literate

Career history

JMF Training Consortium, 2010 – present
Training Supervisor
Trained Community Project volunteers in basic engineering skills for a variety of projects including environmental and conservation work.

G&T Tower Ltd, 2004–2010
Industrial Engineer
Responsible for all industrial engineering services at factory and divisional level. Monitored, coordinated and delivered production engineering service with particular emphasis on product costing, value engineering, pre-production engineering and methods improvement. Provided work-measurement facilities and maintained bonus scheme.

APT Engineering Ltd, 1996–2004
Director/Partner
Planned, organised and implemented all aspects of running a small engineering company.

Pearl Valves Ltd, 1991–1996
Foreman Supervisor
Managed day-to-day control of production lines on a two-shift system. Supervised leading hands, setters and operatives, production planning, quality assurance, coordination of tools and materials and bonus scheme administration.

Promoted to position after joining company in 1981.

Education and training

2010: CRO Training Services
City & Guilds Training for Trainers Certificate

2009: Open University
The Effective Manager

1989–1991: Keyfield College
City & Guilds Certificate in Mechanical Engineering

North East College, supplementary certificates:
Toolroom Practices
Inspection and Quality Assurances
Health and Safety Planning

In-work training, internal and external courses:
Accountancy Part I & II
Team management skills
Negotiation skills
Computer Smartware II
Spreadsheets
Word processing

Personal details

Date of birth: 9 March 1971

Driving licence: Full, clean UK licence, advanced motorist's certificate

Interests: Computers and computing, conservation (I am a member of the local environmental and conservation group), current affairs, swimming.

References: Available on request.

DIANE WALKER
83 Draycot Place
Eastley, Surrey SR1 2AA
Telephone: 0000 0000000

Career profile

An experienced administrator and office manager with an extensive knowledge of business practices especially in accounting, bookkeeping and inventory control.

Key strengths

Excellent IT and administrative skills: currently completing NVQ level 3 course to upgrade administrative and office management skills as well as IT skills. Experienced user of Microsoft Office and Windows XP across a range of functions.

Attention to detail: in my last position, I was responsible for administration of all purchase and inventory documentation and records, requiring a high degree of organisation and attention to detail. Previously I was responsible for analysing and rectifying errors in customer' accounts, which also required an excellent eye for detail.

Ability to supervise staff: have supervised a total of eight staff in a busy retail environment and have also been trained to NVQ level 3 in Supervision.

Key skills

- Supervising staff
- Implementing standard procedures accurately
- Prioritising workload
- Analysing and rectifying errors
- Conversational French
- Computer skills: Word, Excel, Access

Career history

2010 – present: Eastley Training Centre
   NVQ level 3 Clerical Skills Course, Administration and Supervision. Advanced course to update and expand office management skills

2001–2009: Friends Assurance Association
Office Administrator
Responsible for all documentation and records. Also dealt with queries, and the organisation of data within the department

1997–2001: Keyline Retail
Section Manager
Supervised staff and attended to customers in busy city centre store. Responsible for daily administration of section including stock control, turnover, and complaints

1993–1997: Scottish Finance Co.
Office Administrator
Analysed and rectified accounting errors in customer accounts

1990–1993: United Insurance Ltd
Office Administrator
Carried out administrative work of department including invoicing and ordering. Processed payroll and coordinated work schedules

Education and training

2010 – present: Eastley Training Centre
NVQ level 3
Clerical Skills Course concentrating on administration and supervision. This advanced course updates and expands my current office management skills, and also covers Information Technology.

1990–1991: Oldbarrow College of Further Education
College Secretarial Diploma

1985–1990: Impney Court School
GCSEs: seven, including Maths and English
A levels: French, English, Economics

Personal details

Date of birth: 12 December 1972
Health: Non-smoker
Driving licence: Full, clean UK licence
Interests: I work as a dresser for charity fashion shows on a freelance basis at evenings and weekends. This involves being able to keep to a tight timetable, work quickly and accurately, and remain cool, calm and collected under extreme pressure.
References: Available on request.

Chapter Nine
Keeping going

There is now anti-age discrimination law and employers' attitudes *are* changing, but if you are 45 or over, you may wonder how to present yourself in the best light so as to maximise your employment and promotion chances.

Concentrate on the positives. Employers perceive older workers as stable and reliable, mature in their approach, and with good interpersonal skills. Many young people have these qualities too, of course. But one thing older people can offer that younger people may not be able to is experience.

How can you emphasise your experience without filling your CV with a long list of previous jobs?

Career profile

Summarise your career path in the Career profile at the top of your CV. This can speak more fully and persuasively for you than a list of job titles in your Career history section.

Key strengths

Select your skills and experience that match the 'The successful candidate will have ...' statement in the job ad and highlight your suitability for the position. Everything else will be back-up information supporting your application.

Key experience

Rather than a Key skills or Qualifications section, consider including a Key experience section instead. This will clearly emphasise what could be one of your strongest selling points.

Achievements

Demonstrate that your experience brings results and that you have the track record to prove it. Your key achievements can be combined with your key experience, put in a separate section, or clearly listed under your Career history.

Career history

Concentrate on your most recent jobs and edit the rest ruthlessly. For early work, consider simply listing jobs and job titles, and/or grouping jobs together under the heading 'Various'.

Personal details

There is nothing to say you *must* include your date of birth on your CV, and it is up to you whether you include it or not. However, by the time a reader reaches this final section, they should have formed a positive impression of you that will persuade them to consider your application whatever your age.

Examples of CVs appear on the following pages:

Valerie David – continuing as a project manager.

Dominic Hoy – continuing as an electrical engineer.

Alan Bevan – continuing voluntary work after retirement.

Valerie David
17 Three Elms Field
Garby
Stourling HU21 5GN
Tel: 0000 0000000 (home); 0000 0000000 (mobile)

Career profile

A highly trained, confident and effective **project manager** with significant experience in a broad range of construction, manufacturing and industrial projects and proven skills in exploring, designing and implementing solutions and the management of change.

Key strengths

Initiative: my current role as project manager requires highly developed problem-solving skills and the ability to respond to crises swiftly and effectively.

Excellent communication skills: it is essential to liaise effectively with management, technical staff and contractors and to consult with all those actively involved in the project to understand comprehensive user needs and to give information in a way in which it can be understood and assimilated.

Key experience

- Ten years' experience in project management working in a wide range of environments
- Knowledge of health and safety and employment legislation and practice
- An understanding of staff motivation and training
- A clear commitment to excellence
- An established track record in effective solutions

Career history

Bell & Dutton Consultants, 2001 to present
Project Manager
Actively managed a number of projects, including:
Dann Environmental Ltd; Project – Resources and Traffic
Managed traffic flow and resources during development of existing sites
and establishment of new 20-acre industrial site:

- Liaised with external consultants

- Gathered, verified and analysed traffic flow data

- Maintained information flow between departments

Revised site layout and traffic handling patterns, resulting in:

- Expansion and full use of most effective areas

- Elimination of single deliveries in favour of multiple stock drops

- Improved vehicle safety

Whitby Transport Group; Project – Storage and Stock Handling
Developed and improved stock storage and handling system:

- Researched safety regulations

- Devised simplified visual verification system

- Designed and oversaw implementation of new system

Devised and implemented introduction of new storage systems, resulting in:

- Improved stock handling and rotation

- Reduced stock holding

- Safer working practices

- Improved storage facility of flammable and explosive material

The Industrial Training Group Ltd, 1993 to 2001
Training Manager
Managed and administered training projects for agency serving up to 50
local engineering companies:

- Researched opportunities for improvement in services to clients

- Determined supervisory management training needs

Produced comprehensive analysis of training opportunities, skills gaps
and information management systems, resulting in:

- Fully costed training scheme and syllabus

- Effective development and expansion of training group

Various, pre-1993
Management and administrative
A range of managerial and administrative positions for various companies. Responsibilities and achievements over this period include:

- Ensured safe operation of chemical plant during site development
- Increased production turnover of organics at agrochemical company
- Served on safety and work practices committee
- Contributed to operations manual
- Instituted new management control and information systems

Education and training

MBA, Southern School of Business
Diploma in Supervisory Management, Diploma in Operations Management, Cork West College
Computer skills:

CLAIT Certificate in computer literacy

Word

Excel

Outlook

PowerPoint

Personal details

Date of birth: 8 September 1961

Interests: Environmental issues, wildlife and wildlife photography

Health: Non-smoker

Car owner/driver with full, clean UK licence

Dominic Hoy
4 Clements Avenue
High Cross
Berkshire BK17 5LM
Tel: 0000 0000000, e-mail: ddmhoy@anyisp.com

CAREER PROFILE

A skilled and experienced electrical engineer, expert in all aspects of installation, servicing and repair, together with an understanding of staff supervision and management gained in a variety of environments.

KEY SKILLS AND EXPERIENCE

- Over 10 years' experience in electrical engineering
- Knowledge of installing, servicing and repairing electro-mechanical and electronic equipment
- An understanding of precision instrumentation
- An established track record in staff supervision
- A clear commitment to high standards

CAREER HISTORY

2003 to present: Caversham Electrical Engineering
Section Supervisor
Electrical Fitter
Worked in measurement division and repair shop:

- Repaired electronic and electro-mechanical equipment
- Performed or verified precision instrument calibration
- Supervised, administered and coordinated 10 full-time and 3 part-time staff
- Planned work schedules
- Maintained work-sheet records
- Oversaw apprentice training
- Ensured excellent standard of department maintained
- Promoted to Supervisor in 2003

1992 to 2003: Scouts Engineering
Electrical Maintenance Engineer
Worked in maintenance shop and with overhead cranes and hoists:

- Repaired high-speed machine tools
- Serviced overhead equipment
- Overhauled and maintained equipment
- Maintained control equipment
- Performed general electrical maintenance on the site
- Maintained high standards within tight deadlines

Prior to 1992: Various
Electrical Engineer
Responsible for electrical engineering and maintenance in a variety of situations including early experience with electronics and some communications.
Completed apprenticeship in electrical engineering with Abbott Engineering.

EDUCATION AND TRAINING

City & Guilds, Electrical Engineering
Specialist training courses:
Control equipment for high-speed tools
Precision instrument calibration and maintenance

PERSONAL DETAILS

Date of birth: 16 May 1966

Interests: Sailing, studying for Coastal Navigation Certificate, swimming

Health: Non-smoker

Car owner/driver with full, clean UK licence

References available on request

Alan Bevan
50 April Way
Whitpool
Kent KT3 6ZP

Tel: 0000 0000000 (mobile)

CAREER OBJECTIVE

Human resources officer with a fundamental interest in workplace equality together with practical experience of helping young people and those with physical disabilities into rewarding and satisfying employment. Keen to continue using these skills and expertise for the benefit of the community.

KEY STRENGTHS

Organised: currently responsible for HR function for 700 staff across three sites, requiring the highest degree of organisation.

A broad range of personnel skills: 12 years' experience in overall HR function including employment law, union practice, training and development, psychometric testing and performance evaluation systems.

Flexible and adaptable: also created and currently administer voluntary career advice service for people with handicaps. Instrumental in all aspects of the service together with a volunteer staff of seven.

KEY SKILLS AND EXPERIENCE

- Considerable experience in all aspects of human resource assessment and development
- Highly evolved skills in personnel management
- Extensive contacts within training agencies, Training and Enterprise Councils, and employers
- Qualified and experienced in the use of psychometric and aptitude testing
- Experienced in devising, delivering and assessing training courses
- Thorough knowledge of employment law

CAREER HISTORY

2004 to present
Perryman Goldley
Human Resources Manager

- Overall personnel function for office and general staff
- Developed personnel policies and procedures for financial group
- Improved effectiveness of human resource development strategies
- Managed introduction of performance evaluation system

Life Line
2010 to present
Voluntary helper

- Set up and administered career advice and job search service for young people with physical handicaps
- Represented Life Line at the Business Network Forum to promote equality in the workplace
- Liaised with local TEC and FEFC for education and training opportunities and funding

Terrence Parnell Co Ltd
1993 to 2004
Personnel Officer

- Complete personnel function for Head Office and Southern Region Staff
- Administered records, pay and contractual documents
- Promoted from assistant personnel officer in 1989

Fleet Industrial
1983 to 1993
Personnel Assistant, Clerical Officer, Clerical Assistant
Previous clerical and administrative experience gained in a variety of roles between leaving Fieldhouse College and joining Fleet Industrial.

EDUCATION AND TRAINING

Fellow of the Institute of Personnel and Development
Diploma in Personnel Management, Lincoln Business School
Diploma in Education, Fieldhouse College

WORK-RELATED TRAINING

Psychometric testing
Aptitude testing
Assessment skills
Careers guidance and counselling

PERSONAL DETAILS

Date of birth	14 March 1963
Interests	Photography, fell-walking – active member and secretary of Sindon Lake Walkers' Club

Car owner/driver with full, clean UK licence

References available on request

Chapter Ten
CVs for practical jobs

The key thing the employer wants to know:
Are you reliable?

Organisations depend on trustworthy people doing practical jobs reliably. If jobs such as building maintenance, security, deliveries and the like are not done accurately, effectively and efficiently, other employees will be prevented from carrying out their own work.

A prospective employer reading your CV wants to know that you'll be able to do the job competently and skilfully. Demonstrate clearly that you know what needs to be done and that you know how to do it.

As well as addressing their needs directly in your Key strengths section, the most important areas to emphasise in your CV are your past experience, along with any recognised training you have in this particular skill. These will be a good indication of your ability to perform well in the future.

The key qualities needed for most practical jobs are:

- knowledge and hands-on experience of the job;
- these days, usually, proof of adequate training such as NVQ or City & Guilds qualifications;
- competence and reliability;
- self-reliance *as well as* the ability to follow instructions accurately;
- flexibility.

What will help to get these points across?

Career profile

An idea of the work you have done in the past, the amount of experience you have had and your current position will all be useful information to a potential employer.

If you have personal qualities that are useful in your job, such as patience or confidence in dealing with the public, mention these as well.

Key skills

You may need specific qualifications for some types of practical work – an HGV licence for some sorts of driving, or a Hygiene Certificate for catering jobs. If you have relevant qualifications, put them in this section where they can be clearly seen.

Concentrate too on the practical skills that you need for your job and which have proved useful in the past. Make it clear that you understand what the job requires.

Career history

Emphasise the experience you have gained in each job, and the skills you have developed through doing it. Mention any specific responsibilities you have had.

The examples on the following pages show CVs that make use of some or all of the above points. The Practical CVs:

Mary Weber – Chef.

Robert Morgan – Driver.

Diane Donnelly – Dental hygienist.

Peter Ruckerby – Maintenance worker.

Paul Colston – Warehouse supervisor.

This is the job ad Mary Weber is replying to:

Spa Chef

Copperhill Health Spa has an opening for an experienced chef. Working as part of the Catering team and reporting to the Facilities Manager, you will be responsible for providing a high standard of meals and service to meet the nutritional needs of residents, visitors and Spa staff.

You will be expected to accept full responsibility for all catering services and kitchen management in the absence of the Facility Manager.

A recognised catering/food safety qualification such as NVQ Level 3 or City & Guilds equivalent is required.

This is a demanding role that requires excellent organisational skills and a proven ability to multitask, with experience of working in a medium to large kitchen/restaurant and customer-focused environment; familiarity with ordering and stock control would be an advantage. If you have catering experience within a care environment, so much the better.

If you feel you are the person we are looking for, please send your CV to Beth Rogers at _____.

Turn to the next page to see how Mary has used information in this job ad to give her CV focus and relevance by customising her Career profile and Key strengths sections.

Mary Weber
16 Woodland Road
Little Hadby
Norfolk NF14 9MT
Tel: 00000 000000

Career profile

Thoroughly trained chef with experience in both the care environment and commercial catering and with an understanding of a variety of requirements, from stringent nutritional needs to exceptional standards of preparation and presentation.

Key strengths

Experienced: City & Guilds qualified with seven years' experience in catering, including a hospital environment and a high-quality private catering company.

Excellent organisation and multitasking skills: at present working in a high-volume, high-pressure environment preparing meals to exacting standards requiring a high degree of organisation. Working as part of a team requiring flexibility, adaptability and the ability to multitask in order to keep the kitchen running smoothly and efficiently under all circumstances.

Ordering, stock control and kitchen management experience: currently supervise daily food preparation by a team of 12 including 3 junior assistants. Responsible for maintaining stock control sheets and stock ordering sheets, an exacting task in such a high-volume environment.

Key skills

- City & Guilds 706 1 & 2
- Intermediate Food Hygiene Certificate
- Thorough understanding of health and safety regulations
- Knowledge of chilled meals production
- Experience of therapeutic diet preparation

Career history

2006 to present: St Edwards District Health Care Trust
Chef
Worked as member of team providing full meals service within central kitchen preparation unit for large hospital trust producing 5,000 meals a day:

- Prepared meals for consumption within the Trust and other hospitals and day centres
- Supervised routine food preparation
- Prepared food with regard to special dietary requirements such as diabetic, low salt, low fat, gluten free, etc
- Undertook preparation of food for chilling and distribution
- Packed and presented food effectively and attractively

2000 to 2006: SSB Resources South East
Chef, Assistant Chef
Provided high-quality catering service to staff and visitors for a number of large commercial clients, working both on own initiative and as part of a team:

- Prepared breakfast and lunch for up to 2,500 people per day
- Undertook pastry and some confectionery work
- Delivered hospitality service requiring exceptionally high standards of preparation and presentation

1998 to 2000: Five Mile Hill School
Assistant Canteen Cook
Assisted preparation of lunchtime meals service for 1,750 children and staff including menu choices and food prepared to special requirements

---

Education and training

Norfolk City College (day release)
    City & Guilds 706 Cookery for the Catering Industry Part II
    Intermediate Food Hygiene Certificate

South Eastern College of Technology
    City & Guilds 706 Cookery for the Catering Industry Part I

St Edwards and District Secondary School
    Six GCSEs, including English and Maths

Personal details

Date of birth: 21 February 1978
Health: Non-smoker
Interests: All aspects of conservation – National Trust, World Wide Fund for Nature, RSPB
References available on request

Robert Morgan
Flat 1, Riverside Court
Chiderton
Northumberland NB14 5FL

Tel: 0000 0000000

Career profile

A capable, professional delivery and PCV driver, with an excellent driving record and experience of organising own round. Fully responsible for planning and delivery on own route, as well as proficient at dealing with the public in a confident and friendly manner.

Key strengths

Energetic, enthusiastic and reliable: I am proud of my 100 per cent record of punctuality and attendance in my current job. I am required to transport fragile technical products and confidential waste reliably, and have done so to the complete satisfaction of both clients and management. I'm sure colleagues and supervisors would agree that I am always happy to 'go the extra mile'.

Team player: currently required to organise daily deliveries and weekly timetable between a team of three drivers, which requires planning and negotiation to achieve the most efficient schedule for all concerned. Worked very much as part of the Care Team as a PST driver to give the best possible service to patients.

Multi-drop experience: currently make up to 15 drops a day, with responsibility for route planning and loading accordingly.

Key skills

- Clean current UK driving licence
- PCV licence
- Thorough knowledge of the North East area
- Passenger carrying and multi-drop experience
- Able to plan and prioritise schedules and routes as well as work to instruction
- Smart appearance
- Punctual, healthy, reliable

Career history

2005 to present
Bourne & Thomas Ltd
Delivery Driver

- Planned and carried out multi-drop deliveries
- Collected confidential waste safely
- Transported technical products securely and competently
- Planned and organised daily and weekly schedules in agreement with team of drivers
- Maintained schedules and timetables punctually and reliably

2001–2005
NE Central Healthcare Trust
Patient Services Transport Driver

- Provided driver support for Ring and Ride scheme
- Covered two district hospital outpatient departments, three clinics and three day centres
- Arranged most efficient patient pick-up routes in association with Assistant Transport Controller
- Collected outpatients from home and took to destination
- Assisted special needs patients on and off vehicle

1998 to 2001
Pescod Foods Ltd
Customer Service Driver

- Delivered products in North East area
- Loaded van following order sheet
- Maintained delivery records and logs
- Worked flexible shift system

1996–1998
Various
Provided temporary and emergency cover for general driving and delivery work for agencies.

Education and training

J&B Training (for NE Central Health Trust): Passenger Carrying Vehicle Licence
Allerton Secondary School: Four GCSEs, including Maths and English

Personal details

Date of birth: 6 April 1980
Interests: Jazz and music in general, fell-walking, railway and transport enthusiast
Health: Non-smoker
References: Available on request

Diane Donnelly
Flat 1, 121 East Hadbrook Gardens
London NW12 5TT

Tel: 000 000 00000
e-mail: ddonnelly@anyisp.com

Career profile

A competent, reliable dental hygienist experienced in preventative dental care, with excellent interpersonal skills and a clear understanding of the place of oral hygiene in maintaining dental health. A confident, personable individual with experience of working in both private practice and a busy health centre, capable of making a significant contribution to any practice.

Key strengths

Experienced: I have four years' experience as a dental hygienist working in a busy city dental practice and a health centre offering a full range of dental services. I also have four years' experience as a dental nurse working for a prestigious private practice. During this time I have gained my Diploma in Dental Hygiene and Certificate of Proficiency in Dental Nursing.

Able to put patients at their ease: my current job brings me into contact with a wide range of people of all ages and backgrounds and with a variety of dental needs. I use a wide spectrum of communication and interpersonal skills to negotiate their full cooperation and ensure that their experience is as pleasant and effective as possible.

Key skills

- Assessing patient dental health
- Instructing patients on dental health care
- Demonstrating oral hygiene techniques
- Removing tartar, calculus and plaque
- Effecting preventative dental care procedures such as fissure and pit sealing
- Taking and developing dental X-rays
- Administering local anaesthesia
- Providing temporary dressings
- Removing stitches following dental surgery

Key qualifications and experience

Diploma of Dental Hygiene
Certificate of Proficiency in Dental Nursing

Career summary

The Penn Clinic
2008 to present
Dental Hygienist

Brittain, Rayne & Folks
2006 to 2008
Dental Hygienist

Portway Partners
2001 to 2006
Dental Nurse

Topwell Health Centre
2000 to 2001
Dental Receptionist

Education and training

City Central Dental Hospital
   2003 – Diploma of Dental Hygiene
   2000 – Certificate of Proficiency in Dental Nursing

St James Secondary School
   GCSEs: Five including English and Human Biology

Personal details

Date of birth:	17 October 1984
Health:	Non-smoker
Driving licence:	Full, clean UK licence
Interests:	Theatre and cinema
References:	Available on request

Peter Ruckerby
4 Tiverton Lane
Cresslow Common
Buckinghamshire BK7 2WW

Tel: 0000 0000000

Career profile

A versatile, reliable groundsman, gardener and maintenance operative with experience of delivering professional maintenance services for first-class contractors. Proficient at planning own schedules and working on own initiative as well as being able to follow instructions accurately. Hardworking and trustworthy, with the proven ability to remain good-humoured and unflappable under pressure.

Key skills

- Institute of Groundsmanship Qualified
- Five years' experience with established maintenance company
- Experience of recreational and sports grounds maintenance
- Full clean UK driving licence
- Able to work 'on call' rota

Career history

2007 to present: Cornwallis Building & Maintenance Contractors
Maintenance Operative
Provided a top-quality maintenance service to a variety of clients in the Buckinghamshire area. Work undertaken included:

- Basic daily maintenance and preventative repair of properties
- Routine building improvements and repairs
- Carpentry
- Painting and decorating
- Completed service and maintenance logs for each site

Groundsman

Carried out grounds maintenance for two sites. Work undertaken included:

- General seasonal maintenance of grounds
- Maintenance duties:
  - Mowing, rolling and marking
  - Use of pesticides and fertilisers
  - Use of machinery, tools and plant
  - Use of ride-on and gang mower
- Horticultural duties:
  - Tree and shrub planting and pruning
  - Turfing
  - Propagating, planting and plant husbandry

2003 to 2007: South Berkshire and District Leisure Department
Groundsworker Manual 3

1999 to 2003: Hayes & Heartcliffe Environmental Services
Groundsworker Manual 1

Education and training

North Buckinghamshire College of Education
Institute of Groundsmanship: National Practical Certificate

1991–1996 Clevedon School
GCSEs: Five including Maths and English

Personal details

Date of birth:	18 January 1980
Health:	Non-smoker
Interests:	Squash, swimming. Member of the local rugby team
Driving licence:	Full, clean UK licence
References:	Available on request

Paul Colston
71 East Gate
Hadworth
York YK7 4DP
Tel: 0000 0000000
e-mail: pcolston@anyisp.com

Career profile

A logical and methodical warehouse supervisor with an excellent health and safety record and experience of both warehousing and counter service. An adaptable team worker also willing and able to take responsibility for efficient team productivity.

Key strengths

Working knowledge of warehouse management: seven years' experience of warehousing; currently manage and support the Inventory Record Accuracy (IRA) system and the IRA team supplying four sites to ensure stocks of materials are correct and present before production to prevent line downtime and support OEE improvements.

Supervisory skills: currently achieve all departmental and site KPIs by implementing policies and procedures that ensure the department functions in an efficient manner in line with agreed KPIs. Monitor the performance of 15 staff to identify training needs and increase productivity. Encourage and promote good team spirit.

Key skills

Experienced in all aspects of receiving, storing, retrieving and sending out goods:

- Supervising up to 15 staff and checking goods in and out
- Arranging most efficient use of storage locations
- Order picking and assembling:
  - working from order sheets
  - noting inconsistencies
  - checking state of stock
  - reordering as necessary

- Packing and dispatching:
  - assembling orders
  - preparing for transport – postage or delivery
- Storekeeping:
  - selling parts as trade counter assistant
  - maintaining computerised record system
  - using computer terminal and checking printouts to assess availability of parts

Career summary

2007 to present: Auto City Supplies Ltd – **Warehouse Supervisor, Warehouse worker**

2003 to 2007: Northern Stores Ltd – **Warehouse Worker**

2001 to 2003: H Pearson McDuff – **Warehouse Worker, Shelf Stacker**

2000 to 2001: Various – **Shelf Stacker, General Assistant**

Education and training

South Yorkshire College (day release)
   NVQ level 2 – Wholesaling, Warehousing and Stores
   NVQ level 1 – Wholesaling, Warehousing and Stores
Edmund Fairview School
   Six GCSEs, including Maths

Personal details

Date of birth: 9 June 1984

Driving licence: Full, clean UK licence

Interests: All team sports. Captain of Hadworth and District Cricket Team

References available on request

Chapter Eleven
CVs for creative jobs

The key thing the employer wants to know:
Will you deliver?

Creative people provide solutions to problems.
It's the creative person's job to use their technical skill and expertise – in design, graphics, engineering or whatever – to achieve tangible results with originality and flair.

Most creative vacancies will require evidence of your creative skills by way of a portfolio of examples. It's important that your CV puts these creative skills in context and emphasises your ability to deliver work of a similar quality, reliably and professionally. The most important area to emphasise, therefore, is your past experience of doing this, which will be a good indication of your ability to do so again in the future.

The key qualities employers usually require in creative personnel are:

- a thorough understanding of your specific field;
- the ability to come up with effective solutions to problems;
- competence and dependably high standards;
- the ability to work both individually *and* with a team to achieve results;
- flexibility, energy and enthusiasm.

What will get these characteristics across to a prospective employer?

Career profile

An idea of what you have done and how you have done it will be useful in assessing your knowledge and experience.

Key experience

Technical and practical competence and experience are key requirements in creative jobs; it's only when they are present that style and originality can develop. Outline the range of skills you have, and expand on your achievements. This will help an employer to assess your probable future performance.

Career history

Your experience of encountering and solving problems is important. Give details of the skills you have developed in different jobs.

The examples that follow show creative CVs that include a Key experience section, and make use of some or all of the above points. The Creative CVs:

Rosa Devon – Interior and exhibition designer.

Alan Moorhouse – Writer and broadcaster.

Hannah Gansa – Editorial assistant and photographer.

Luke Jump – Graphic artist.

Barbra Kingdom – Video maker.

This is the job that Rosa Devon is applying for:

Interior Designer (mid-weight)

London-based Design Company specialising in furniture, products and interiors is looking to hire an Interior Designer who would be able to work with flexibility on a diverse range of design projects.

The ideal candidate will have a strong knowledge of interior design and project management, including liaising with clients and vendors, producing specification documents, overseeing construction administration, and managing a team (two to three years' experience preferable).

Computer skills will include AutoCAD, Graphite, Adobe Creative Suite, Microsoft Office.

Model-making skills are required, as is the ability to create presentation documents for client presentations.

Reply with CV to Paul Hodge at _____

See how Rosa used this job ad to target her CV on the next page.

Rosa Devon
31 Verdon Villas
Spring Gate Heath
Essex EX12 7YC
Tel. 0000 0000000
E-mail: rdevon@anyisp.com

Career profile:

An experienced designer with a background in retail display and domestic design, and a sound understanding of detailed specification, planning and budgeting, and liaising with both clients and subcontractors.

Key skills:

Knowledge of interior design/project management: designed and managed 10 medium- to large-scale projects to a high degree of client satisfaction. Adept at liaising with clients, suppliers and local contractors. Previously, six years' experience heading team designing and installing showroom exhibitions for a major furniture retailer.

Flexible: responsible for a wide variety of projects including listed buildings, show homes, a pleasure cruiser and a children's day centre. Flexible and adaptable in order to bring diverse projects in on time and to budget. Experienced at working to a range of budgets and client considerations, and enjoy the challenge of the unexpected.

Computer skills: AutoCAD, Graphite, Adobe Creative Suite, Microsoft Office. I also have experience of 3-D model-making.

Key experience:

- Overall management of refurbishment of specialist retail outlet, having responsibility for:
  - design
  - planning
  - budgeting
  - materials specification
  - purchasing
  - hiring subcontractors
- Successfully designing and planning over two dozen shop-floor and point-of-sale exhibitions for a home-furnishing retail chain
- Establishing a successful interior design service in conjunction with a local furnishing store
- Designing, specifying and supervising interior renovation of two Grade II listed properties in heritage area
- Bringing the project in on budget and contributing to a £100k profit for the developer

---

Career history:

2006 to present: Self-employed
Designer and Decorator
Designed domestic and retail interiors:

- Assessed client requirements
- Negotiated fees and budget with client
- Selected suitable wall coverings, furnishings and fabrics
- Presented proposals to clients
- Bought from UK and overseas sources
- Created specialist decorative paint finishes
- Liaised between client and subcontractors
- Worked to pre-agreed timescale and budget

2001 to 2006: Marc D'Araby Furniture Galleries Ltd
Display Designer
Designed showroom and point-of-sale displays for retail chain throughout the South of England:

- Assessed requirements of individual store managers
- Designed 'customer-friendly' display settings
- Drew up fully detailed plans and instructions for installation by local contractors
- Supervised final stages and set dressing
- Maintained, renovated and updated displays

1996 to 2001: Sollways of Liverpool
Display Designer, Window Dresser
Undertook window dressing, in-store display and promotion of home and garden products as part of display team for large city-centre department store. Promoted to Display Designer in 1996.

Education and training:

1994 to 1996: City College
Retail Display Certificate Course
Marketing and Retailing
Retail and Retail Display
Point-of-Sale Merchandising
Advertising and Promotion

1990 to 1994: East Faringdean School
Five GCSEs, including Maths and English

Personal details:

Date of birth: 8 June 1978

Interests: Member of the South of England Watercolour Society and the Women Mean Business Club. Enjoy dancing and antique collecting

Car owner/driver with full, clean UK licence

Alan Moorhouse
23 The Avenue
Seaton Parva
Hampshire HA3 6TL
Tel: 0000 0000000

Career profile

A writer and broadcaster with a total of 15 years' experience, including 7 years as a regular contributor to Radio Hampshire. An effective communicator with a track record of successful books, articles and radio pieces on local history and regional issues, based on a thorough understanding of journalism.

Key experience

Writing:

- Researching and writing *Buckler's Hard* – the story of Henry Adams, Nelson's shipbuilder
- Compiling three local guidebooks:
  - *Romsey Rambles*
  - *Winchester Wanders*
  - *Portsmouth Parade*
- Editing Tourist Board publications:
  - *Days Out on the South Coast – Portsmouth and District*
  - *Days Out on the South Coast – The New Forest*
- Writing a regular 'Local Heroes' column for *Portsmouth Pickings*
- Contributing over 100 articles on local history and natural history for the *South Hampshire Chronicle* and *Points Around* magazine

Broadcasting:

- Dramatising *Buckler's Hard* for Radio Hampshire
- Broadcasting regular 10- and 20-minute reports on items of local interest on 'Out and About'
- Writing and presenting 30-minute promotional video for Southcrest Hotels, 'Blow the Man Down'

Career history

2003 to present
Freelance Writer
Clients include:

- Hampshire Press Ltd
- Tourist Information Board
- Tourist Services Ltd
- Portsmouth Gazette Publications
- Southcrest Holdings Ltd
- Radio Hampshire
- Daniel Deckland & Co Ltd

2000 to 2003: South Downs Heritage Centre
Publications Manager
Compiled, catalogued and promoted publications of interest to visitors to the Heritage Centre, and for use as a local information resource.

1991 to 2000: *South Hampshire Chronicle*
Features Editor, Reporter
Edited newspaper articles on local events. Researched and wrote regular column. Reported on local issues. Promoted to Features Editor in 1993.

Education and training

1989–1991 College of Trade and Commerce
Diploma in Journalism

1985–1988 South Eastern University
BA History and English

1978–1985 Oversands High School
A levels: English, History, French
GCSEs: eight including English and Maths

Personal details

Date of birth	17 August 1967
Interests	Natural history, Member of South Down Botanical Society, Member of the Tallinger local history group, voluntary tutor on the local literacy initiative scheme

Car owner/driver with full, clean UK licence

References available on request

Hannah Gansa
Flat 4, Tily Court Mansions
London SW9 0PP

Tel: 0000 000000
e-mail: hgansa@fairport.co.uk

CAREER PROFILE

An experienced assistant editor and photographer with a background in specialist craft books and magazines. Possessing a high degree of technical competence and a commitment to quality, I am now looking for a challenging position where these can be used to maximum effect.

KEY STRENGTHS

Commitment to quality: currently responsible for commissioning the high-quality graphics for which field leader Fairport Magazines is known; instrumental in team that won the Publishing Award two years running.

People skills: have worked profitably with a wide range of people, liaising successfully with editors, suppliers, authors and freelance contributors. Able to question, consult, negotiate and influence to gain understanding of the client's needs using a wide spectrum of approaches to ensure that both editors and contributors feel happy with the outcome.

KEY EXPERIENCE AND ACHIEVEMENTS

- Planning and implementing visual policy for two leading magazines
- Developing key areas within the subject field
- Winning 'Craft Magazine of the Year' two years in succession
- Successfully implementing editorial policy
- Liaising tactfully with authors and freelance contributors
- Designing and co-writing promotional material
- Coordinating public relations, publicity and press releases

CAREER HISTORY

2008 to present: **Fairport Magazines Ltd**
Needles and Threads, Happy Hands
Assistant Editor/Photographer
Designed and organised photographs and photographic policy for the magazines:

- Designed, set up and photographed spreads
- Organised and photographed 'step-by-step' instruction series in conjunction with craftspeople
- Edited freelance submissions to journal standard
- Researched and developed new fields of interest to readership
- Solicited contributions from craftworkers
- Covered exhibitions and conventions for news items, ideas and information
- Organised and carried out interviews and photographic sessions with subjects

2004 to 2008: **Cotswolds Crafts Publications Ltd**
Editorial Assistant
Prepared written material for publication:

- Reviewed copy for errors in spelling, syntax and punctuation
- Ensured manuscripts conformed to house style and editorial policy
- Conferred with authors regarding copy changes
- Marked copy for typesetting using standard symbols
- Selected and prepared photographs and illustrations

2001 to 2004: **Berholt Freeman Ltd**
Marketing Assistant
Assisted with company marketing and promotion:

- Produced annual report, press releases, newsletter and brochures
- Liaised with ad agencies, printers, art directors, audio-visual and video producers
- Coordinated public relations exercises
- Organised inclusion in exhibitions and trade shows

1999 to 2001: Dollar Holdings
Secretary to Marketing Department

- Provided secretarial cover for the department
- Assisted marketing personnel where appropriate

EDUCATION AND TRAINING

Three Acres College of Art and Technology, 2006 to 2008 (part-time)
    Certificate of Photographic Studies

Sperring Sixth Form College/CFE, 1994 to 1996
    RSA II Secretarial Certificate
    A levels – English, Art, French

Turnall Secondary School, 1992 to 1997
    GCSEs – six including English and Maths

PERSONAL

Date of birth:	1 May 1981
Health:	Non-smoker
Driving licence:	Full, clean UK licence
Interests:	Member of local amateur orchestra, music appreciation, swimming, aromatherapy
References:	Available on request

Luke Jump
56 Ballard Place
Ashworthy
Oxfordshire OX14 5LA

Tel: 0000 0000000; e-mail: ljump@brand.co.uk

Career profile

Experienced graphic artist with the proven ability to understand client requirements and deliver effective creative solutions within specified deadlines, the ability to use modern technology in the production of graphic material and a wide range of traditional skills, along with well-developed communication skills honed by extensive dealings with senior management and other professionals.

Key skills

Creative drive: successful and award-winning campaigns include 'Beat the Clock' for Em Kay, 'Up and Running' for Game+, 'Pop-pop' for PeopleNet, and 'Ticket to Write' for ESC. Director of Media Standard award agency.

Leadership skills: track record of eight years of motivating an award-winning team to establish and achieve challenging goals and demand the very best from themselves. Feedback from teams demonstrates a confident, vigorous style of leadership based on sincere consultation allied with vision and clear direction.

Communication skills: extensive experience of consultation with client companies; personally conduct client presentations; negotiate with suppliers; consult with team and freelance staff.

Key experience

- Working with Macintosh graphics packages:
  - Quark Xpress
  - Illustrator
  - Photoshop
- Working with four-colour reproduction
- Liaising, consulting and negotiating with clients, including:
  - LLK
  - Employment Services Commission
  - Playnet Computers
  - Kase UK
- Art director of agency winning 'Media Standard' award 2006 and 2008

Career history

2009 – present
Brand Response
Art Director
Devised concepts and supervised staff in preparing layout designs for artwork and copy for direct marketing agency:

- Consulted with client companies on aims and objectives, presentation and budget
- Formulated layout and design concept
- Produced, selected or arranged to have produced suitable material for artwork and/or illustrations
- Supervised staff preparing layouts for printing
- Approved final layout for presentation to client

2007–2009
Wells Strata Deanery
Assistant Studio Manager
Assisted organisation and running of studio together with production of high-grade computer graphics for audio-visual company:

- Created a range of graphics for flipcharts, OHP, 35 mm, video presentations and slide animations
- Supervised allocation of projects
- Briefed and monitored freelance staff

News Review Publications Ltd
2005–2007
Designer
Produced graphic material for company bulletins, brochures, annual reports and in-house magazines.

PAC Magazines Ltd
2004–2005
Paste-up Artist
Produced paste-ups and mechanicals for magazines

Education and training

Work-related training:
  Quark Xpress
  Photoshop
  Illustrator

South Counties College of Art and Design, 2000–2003
Diploma in Art and Design

John Galliard School, 1993–2000
A levels – English, Art
GCSEs – six including English and Technical Drawing

Personal details

Date of birth: 16 September 1982

Driving licence: Full, clean UK licence

Interests: Marathon running, swimming, hill walking and climbing

References: Available on request

Barbra Kingdom
41A Pine Court Gardens
Landschurch
Avon AV5 1MR
Tel: 0000 0000000
e-mail: bkingdom@anyisp.com

Career profile:

Innovative and intelligent video maker with experience gained designing and producing videos for a broad range of clients. Adept at working with a wide variety of people effectively and good-humouredly in sometimes demanding situations. Skilled at evaluating and resolving problems creatively.

Key strengths:

Working with people: have worked successfully with a wide range of people, including some quite challenging groups. Able to question, consult, negotiate and influence to gain understanding of the client's needs using a wide spectrum of approaches to ensure that the client feels happy with the outcome.

Technical expertise: comprehensive practical experience based on HND Media and Visual studies training. For full range of expertise – please see below.

Key experience:

Video and Film

- Producing and directing seven 30- to 60-minute videos for The Parenting Initiative, including 'Baby Talk', 'Little White Lies' and 'Babyland'
- Deciding with featured expert the content and presentation of the topic on video
- Planning lighting, camera angles, camera shots
- Assisting youth group making youth and community videos
- Training them in use of equipment and basic production and editing
- Designing, producing and directing two independent video shorts, 'Moon' and 'All Sorts', shown at the Arts South West Film Festival

Editing

- Machine-to-machine video editing
- Digital and online editing
- Coordinating sound, content and storyline
- Dubbing
- Super-8 film viewing, editing and splicing

Radio

- Researching, planning and presenting weekly community arts slot on local radio
- Delivering reports
- Selecting, approaching and interviewing guests

Career history:

2003 to present
Video Maker, Community Production Facility
Radio Producer and Presenter, Valley Radio
Video Trainer/Facilitator, Kids TV, Community Youth Group

Education and training:

2002–2006 Wessex College of Art and Technology
    BTEC HND Media and Visual Studies
Vocational studies:
    The Moving Image
    Twentieth Century Film
    The National Film Archive

1995–2001 East Faringdean School
    GCSEs – five, including English Language
    A levels – English and Art

Personal details:

Date of birth: 15 September 1984

Interests: Film, video and music

Car owner/driver with full, clean UK licence

References: available on request

Chapter Twelve
CVs for clerical and administrative jobs

The key thing the employer wants to know:
Are you efficient?

Clerks and administrators ensure that an organisation runs smoothly and efficiently. It's important that a prospective employer reading your CV believes that you will, first and foremost, take over the vacancy smoothly, effectively and as proficiently as possible, with very little disruption to the department. As well as specifically addressing the needs stated in the job ad, the most important areas to emphasise are your current skills and past experience as these will be the best guide to your future performance.

The key qualities employers usually look for in applicants for clerical and administrative jobs are:

- organisation;
- dependability;
- a methodical approach;
- the ability to work with others;
- specific technical skills;
- experience in specific areas.

What are the main points, then, for a clerical and administrative CV?

Key skills

Many clerical, administrative and secretarial jobs call for specific skills such as word-processing or bookkeeping skills, use of a particular sort of switchboard, use of particular computer software packages or knowledge of a specific language.

Include all your relevant skills, and highlight the specific skills required for the position in your Key skills section so that they can be clearly seen.

Key experience

Experience in a specific field is often a job requirement – a computer services administrator will have a different area of knowledge and expertise from a personnel administrator. Include experience such as supervision and planning that will be relevant to most positions, then choose Key experience – payroll procedures, customer services, whatever – to fit the job you are applying for.

Career history

Concentrate on areas of responsibility, skills used and experience gained. Include improvements in departmental efficiency you have introduced.

Some people find that their clerical or administrative jobs have been essentially similar in content. In this case concentrate on emphasising Key skills and Key experience and simply summarise your actual Career history.

The examples on the following pages show CVs that include both Key skills and a Key experience sections that make use of some or all of these points.

The Administrative CVs:

Amanda Barwell – Clerical assistant.

Tessa Dixon – Secretary.

Valerie Andrews – Secretarial and financial administrator.

Philip McVickery – Information technology administrator.

Rose Mary Tan – Records administrator.

This is the ad that Amanda Barwell is replying to:

Are you an experienced Accounts Clerk?

Do you have outstanding clerical and computer skills?
Do you want to work for a small, friendly, successful company?

Our city centre client is looking for an experienced Accounts Clerk. The role requires previous accounts office experience and will involve preparing accounts, processing and coding invoices, raising and receipting purchase orders, processing invoice payments, period end including prepayments and accruals, preparing profit and loss reports, and dealing with any variances.

The successful candidate will have solid office experience and a professional, confident manner.

This is a great opportunity to work for a successful company in a much-sought-after location.

Reply with your CV to _____.

Amanda Barwell used this job ad to customise her CV so that her suitability for the job would be hard to overlook. She shows how she achieved this on the next page.

Amanda Barwell
5 Juniper Court
Nine Trees
Devon DV22 1JC
Tel: 0000 0000000

Career profile:

Experienced City & Guilds-qualified Accounts Clerk with a comprehensive range of accounts skills and experience of order office and general office administration.

Key strengths:

Outstanding clerical and computer skills: C&G 8953 1 & 2 qualified with five years' experience. Advanced Excel and Access skills; some Sage experience. Comprehensive training in Microsoft Office.

Solid office experience: currently Accounts Clerk for the Languages Department of a large higher education college, undertaking a full range of duties and responsibilities including all those mentioned in the job advertisement. Previously I was an Order Clerk for a busy contracts company responsible for orders and invoicing, and I have several years' experience in other clerical roles.

Professional, confident manner: required to liaise with other departments and members of staff to a very high level, as well as with suppliers and contractors.

Key skills:

- preparing accounts
- preparing statements showing income and expenditure
- processing sales invoices, receipts and payments
- checking that accounts are accurate and dealing with variances
- helping to prepare final accounts, profit and loss accounts and balance sheets
- using computerised accounting systems
- providing administrative support to accountants

Key experience:

Accounts clerk

- documenting accounts
- preparing correspondence
- processing invoices, cheques, credit and debit notes, payments and receipts
- inputting data onto computer files

Order clerk

- processing orders
- raising order codes
- preparing dockets and dispatching emergency orders
- filing and retrieving dispatch notes, orders and delivery records

Clerk-typist

- typing from manuscript – 40 wpm
- completing and dispatching reports
- maintaining files
- organising appointments
- cover for reception and switchboard

Career history:

2006 to present, Kellington Park College: **Accounts clerk**

2004 to 2006, West End Office Contracts Ltd: **Order Clerk**

2003 to 2004, Dobson Dean & Co Ltd: **Clerk-Typist**

2001 to 2003, Hindway Ltd: **Clerical Assistant**

1999 to 2001, Southcross Hospital: **Clerical Assistant**

Education:

2006 to 2008, East Devon Open Learning Centre
    Microsoft Office
    Pitman Intermediate Office Practice

2003 to 2005, Whitcombe College
    City & Guilds, 8953 1 & 2

1994 to 1999, Marsh Cross School
    Seven GCSEs, including Maths, English and Commerce

Personal details:

Date of birth: 19 January 1983

Interests: Aerobics, swimming and walking

Full, clean UK driving licence

References available on request

Tessa Dixon
61 Chantry Hill
Stoke Dean, Essex EX3 5DM
Tel: 0000 0000000
e-mail: tdixon@anyisp.com

Career profile

A highly trained and experienced personal secretary with excellent shorthand and word-processing skills, who has developed, as secretary to the Managing Director of a prominent property company, first-rate organisational skills and initiative.

Key strengths

Executive support experience: currently confidential secretary to Managing Director; previously personal secretary to Head of Section; five years' executive-level experience in total.

Excellent secretarial skills: 10 years' experience working in professional corporate environments, providing full secretarial support including diary management, dealing with overseas clients and screening calls and e-mails; advanced skills in Word, Excel and PowerPoint; good working knowledge of Lotus Notes.

Key skills

Secretarial skills:

- Pitman Private Secretary Diploma
- Keyboard – 70 wpm
- Shorthand – 120 wpm
- Audio typing
- Commercial correspondence

Computer skills:

- Word
- Outlook Express
- Excel
- Access
- PowerPoint

Experience

- Ten years' secretarial experience in a wide range of environments
- An understanding of business and the secretary's role therein
- A clear commitment to efficiency
- Knowledge of good office practice and procedures
- An established track record in effective office support

Career summary

2008 to present
Heath McIllany Properties
Confidential Secretary
Provided full secretarial support:

- Typed letters, memoranda and reports with due regard to confidentiality
- Compiled monthly reports and statistics
- Organised meetings, took and typed minutes
- Arranged accommodation and travel for staff and overseas visitors
- Coordinated diary and appointments for MD
- Communicated with overseas clients

2006 to 2008
Dockland Industrial Company
Personal Secretary
Provided secretarial support to head of section:

- Arranged internal and external meetings
- Took minutes at meetings and typed them up along with summaries and reports for other departments
- Organised all resulting correspondence and enquiries
- Liaised with outside agencies in the production of reports

2004 to 2006
Timberland Insurance
Department Secretary
Provided secretarial support for New Business Team

2001 to 2004
Stanegate Holdings Ltd
Personal Secretary, Shorthand Typist

Education and training

Member of the Institute of Qualified Private Secretaries
2007–2009 City Adult Education College (part-time/evening course)
  Pitman Private Secretary Diploma
  Pitman Commercial Correspondence
  Pitman Shorthand
1999–2001 Westmordale College of Education
  RSA III Typewriting (Distinction)
  RSA III Shorthand and Typewriting Certificate
  RSA III Audio-typing
  RSA II English Language
1993–1998 Clevedon School
  GCSEs: Five including Maths and English

Personal details

Date of birth:	9 October 1982
Health:	Non-smoker
Driving licence:	Full, clean UK licence
Interests:	Theatre and cinema
References:	Available on request

Valerie Andrews
43 Newton Street
Northampton N14 5ET

Tel: 0000 0000000

CAREER PROFILE

A well-organised, reliable secretary with extensive knowledge of good office practice, and a wealth of experience in both large and small companies.

KEY STRENGTHS

Excellent IT and secretarial skills: four years' secretarial experience providing support for two department heads and the Personnel Director; four years' experience managing the administrative side of a busy sales office. College trained and fully proficient in Microsoft Office, including Word and Excel; currently using Windows XP.

Communication skills: As Office Manager, good communication skills ensured the smooth and efficient running of the office. Excellent presentation, both verbal and written, required as confidential secretary to the Director along with the ability to liaise effectively with clients and other members of staff in person, by letter and over the phone.

Initiative and flexibility: currently required to prioritise own workload and that of junior staff, and manage administrative organisation effectively. Sales drives and conferences mean working competently and resourcefully under pressure to tight deadlines to meet urgent requirements. Always happy to 'go the extra mile' when necessary.

KEY QUALIFICATIONS

- RSA III Typewriting – current speed 70 wpm
- RSA II Audio-typing – current speed 70 wpm
- RSA II Shorthand – current speed 120 wpm
- City & Guilds CLAIT – Microsoft Office

KEY EXPERIENCE

Secretarial:

- Confidential Secretary to Personnel Director
- Secretary to Finance Manager

- Secretary to Marketing Department
- Preparing reports and correspondence
- Setting up agendas and minuting all departmental meetings
- Organising client presentations and corporate entertainment

Administrative:

- Responsible for day-to-day running of 10-person department
- Answerable for all secretarial staff administration
- Coordinating department work schedules
- Training and supervising junior staff

Financial administration:

- Compiling monthly budget reports
- Preparing quantity audits, projections, and financial statements
- Responsible for raising orders and invoicing for office stationery and consumables
- Supervising accounts payable and accounts receivable

CAREER SUMMARY

2008 to present: Heathfield Enterprises Ltd, Northampton, **Personal Secretary**

2000 to 2008: Somerhill & Hayes Ltd, Ipswich, **Office Manager**

1996 to 2000: Tanstead Personnel Ltd, Preston, **Temporary Secretarial/ Clerical positions**

EDUCATION AND TRAINING

1993–1996 North Preston College of Education
  RSA Secretarial Certificate
  RSA Stage II
  RSA Stage III

1986–1993 Clevedon School
  GCSEs: Five including Maths and English
  A levels: English, French and Commerce

Personal details

Date of birth: 21 April 1975
Health: Non-smoker
Interests: Badminton, swimming, member of the local Operatic Society
References: Available on request

Philip McVickery
66 Cleve Way
St Aldans
Leicestershire LE17 8UK
Tel: 0000 0000000, E-mail: pmcvickery@anyisp.com

CAREER PROFILE

Experienced administrator with budget, IT and premises-management skills and a background in insurance, commerce and not-for-profit sectors. Seeking the opportunity to use IT skills in a company where they can contribute to a worthwhile outcome.

KEY STRENGTHS

Excellent IT skills: gained extensive skills in office applications as systems controller maintaining IT facilities. Currently use Microsoft Office.

Initiative: devised and implemented clear administrative procedures for the Trust's office so that information could be filed and retrieved efficiently; traced and acted upon all outstanding bills and invoices, clarifying the financial position; rationalised entry of information onto database with the result that the Trust's business was more accurately represented.

KEY QUALIFICATIONS

- Finance for Administrators:
  - Budgeting for contract tenders for government funding
  - Budgeting to precise figures
- Computer skills:
  - JSP structured programme design
  - VAX 780 computer system
  - Excel and SuperCalc spreadsheet applications
  - Access database
  - Microsoft Word word processing

KEY SKILLS

- Understanding and using information technology
- Interpreting instructions and carrying out policies accurately
- Dealing with people effectively, tactfully and efficiently
- Analysing problems and providing solutions
- Planning work to meet deadlines

CAREER HISTORY

2008 – present: **Keyline Youth Trust – Administrator**
Ran administrative department on a day-to-day basis, including:

- Budget control and petty cash
- Premises management
- Designed and implemented administrative procedures in office
- Traced and acted upon all outstanding bills and invoices
- Rationalised entry of information onto database with the result that the Trust's business was more accurately represented

2003–2008: **JJ Hey Ltd – System Controller**
Ran computer system for six offices, including:

- Routine hardware maintenance
- Data backup
- Provided help-desk facility
- Facilitated effective staff usage of all computer facilities
- Monitored printing and stationery costs and implemented cost-effective measures

1998–2003: **L&S Insurance – Claims Supervisor**
Assessed claims for redundancy insurance, including:

- Maintained cheque issue deadlines
- Supervised up to seven staff members
- Maintained and administered insurance certificate stocks
- Revised wording of unemployment benefit monthly claim forms resulting in 12% reduction in errors
- Established criteria for conversion of clerical claims to computer operation, resulting in minimal disruption for clients

1992–1997: **Department of Employment – Clerical Officer**
Processed claims for unemployment benefit

EDUCATION AND TRAINING

1987–1991 Chesterfield College of Education
   Certificate of Education: Education Theory, English and Drama
1980–1987 Tembury South School
   GCSEs: Five including Maths and English
   A levels: English and Art

PERSONAL DETAILS

Date of birth: 9 February 1969

References: Available on request

Rose Mary Tan
4A Sandle Lane
Churchdean
Dorset DR12 3BL
Tel: 0000 0000000

Career profile

A thorough and methodical records administrator, with extensive experience in the verification, storage and retrieval of records both as documents and on computer databases.

Key strengths

Excellent IT skills: comprehensively trained and experienced in all aspects of database and records systems – collection, storage and retrieval as well as first-stage statistical analysis. Currently using Windows XP office applications.

Supervisory skills: currently supervise 10 staff in records administration including induction and training. Devised and implemented new strategy for handling high volumes of data and trained staff accordingly, leading to a substantial decrease in errors and omissions.

Accuracy and attention to detail: retrieve and administer a large volume of medical data and documents, requiring a high degree of accuracy if comprehensive patient records are to be maintained. All inconsistencies are queried and there has been no substantiated complaint in my department in 18 months.

Key qualifications

- Database and record systems: Access; Excel; MediWatch tailored statistical package
- Computer skills: Word; Outlook Express

Key skills

- Maintaining, developing and administering medical records and data systems
- Supervising staff compiling and inputting record data, and storing documents
- Collecting, storing and retrieving patient data
- Formulating strategies for handling high-volume records
- Implementing effective procedures for storage and retrieval
- Developing 'user-friendly' methods for staff processing
- Undertaking first-stage statistical analysis
- Preparing and supplying information for staff and departments

Career history

Porterhouse Hospital Trust
2006 – present
Records Administrator
Experienced in all aspects of receiving, storing, retrieving and supplying data:

- Supervised up to 10 staff
- Maintained and updated records and files
- Checked records in and out
- Noted inconsistencies and queried as necessary
- Processed both documents and computerised records and printouts

Fordice Road Health Centre
2002–2006
Administrative Assistant
Provided clerical and administrative support to Centre Administrator:

- Maintained and updated records
- Input and retrieved data and statistical information
- Coordinated communication between staff, clinics and clinic users
- Monitored usage of consumables

Department of Employment
2000–2002
Clerical Officer, Clerical Worker

- Processed claims for unemployment benefit
- Maintained and updated client records

Education and training

Blare Petrie College
  Introduction to Computer Literacy
  Working with Spreadsheets
  Working with Databases: introductory to advanced level; working with
    Windows databases
Torburymouth Senior School
  GCSEs: Five including Maths and English

Personal details

Date of birth: 30 March 1984
Interests: Opera and classical ballet, gardening
References: Available on request

Chapter Thirteen
CVs for sales and marketing jobs

The key thing the employer wants to know: Can you sell?

Salespeople ensure that a company sells its products and makes a profit. Prospective employers reading your CV are looking for confirmation that you will be able to sell their goods or services and increase profits for them. The most important thing to emphasise, therefore, is your past success in doing this.

The key qualities employers usually look for in applicants for sales jobs are:

- the ability to sell;
- tenacity and perseverance;
- competence;
- the ability to get on with others;
- energy, commitment and enthusiasm.

What will help you get these points across?

Career profile

An idea of the areas you have covered in the past, the sort of experience you have had to date and your current position in your career will all be helpful information to a potential employer.

If you have experience outside sales but relevant to the job you are applying for, include it. Buyers like to feel they are dealing with someone who understands what they're talking about.

Key achievements

Companies want salespeople who can work hard and make money. Let them know what you're capable of doing. If you regularly exceed targets, have a habit of increasing profits or always get the most orders, make sure they know about it.

Career history

This is where you can put actual facts and figures to the claims you have made about your achievements. Outline your performance with past companies and expand on your successes, rather than just stating your responsibilities.

The examples on the following pages show CVs that make use of some or all of the above points, including a Key achievements section. The sales and Marketing CVs:

Linda Knauf – Telesales.

Paul A Hendry – Retail store manager.

Paige McLeod – Salesperson and sales manager.

Francis Scott – Sales/product manager.

Ruth Sefton – Media executive.

This is the job that Linda Knauf is applying for:

Experienced Telesales Executive

Our company is one of the UK's leading providers of premier office equipment and we are currently seeking someone with unusually good telesales skills.

You will be responsible for undertaking a range of duties required to ensure the ongoing development and maintenance of the company, including cold-calling prospective clients ranging from small enterprises to blue-chip organisations, booking appointments, reaching weekly targets set by the Sales Manager, following up appointments and re-appointing where necessary.

You will have relevant experience in an equivalent telesales role, be organised, proactive and systematic, and have excellent interpersonal skills and an articulate and friendly telephone manner.

It goes without saying that you are a dedicated team player with drive and initiative.

If this sounds like you, reply with your CV to _____.

Linda answered this ad with the CV on the next page. She used the information it contained to tailor her Career profile and Key strengths to show her suitability for the job.

Linda Knauf
Flat 4, 115 Trebarton Road
Colby
Bucks BK11 7CW
Tel: 0000 0000000

Career profile:

Trained telesales professional with eight years' experience selling premier products and services to business and the public.

Key strengths:

Organised, proactive and systematic: achieved results 15 per cent above target by devising and developing an organised, systematic approach that meant every new customer was contacted and all return customers approached after three months for optimum results.

Excellent interpersonal skills: regularly turned negative responses into positive ones using a comprehensive spectrum of skills; achieved highest rate of return business in the company.

Drive and initiative: have achieved steady promotion with each job through self-funded training and the determination to achieve outstanding results. Have devised several initiatives and innovations subsequently adopted by the rest of the team.

Key achievements:

- Consistently meeting and exceeding targets by 10–15%
- Achieving 110% increase in sales for new territory
- Winning 'top team' award for home improvement sales
- Successfully combining customer care service with new business development programme
- Achieving NVQ 2 in Telephone Selling:
  - Gaining customer attention and interest
  - Projecting company image effectively
  - Winning appointments
  - Handling objections positively and professionally

Career history:

2008 to present, Auto Credit Europe plc: **Telesales/Aftercare service**

- Advised customers how to finance their car purchase
- Negotiated with all types of customers
- Worked effectively with field sales team
- Achieved weekly average sales of £25K worth of cover
- Optimised profit opportunities and sales performance, contributing to an overall centre sales increase of 10%
- Increased sales of financial packages and add-on products by 17%

2006 to 2008, Redhouse Publications: **Advertisement sales**

- Successfully sold advertising space for two best-selling computer magazines
- Operated in a highly competitive environment
- Achieved 15% increase in sales over and above target

2004 to 2006, Laurell Communications Ltd: **Telesales**

- Effectively sold mobile communications systems to businesses
- Assisted in building up new territory in South Midlands
- Achieved 110% new business growth in first year, 40% ahead of target

2003 to 2004, Wallmix Ltd: **Telesales**

- Cold-called to arranged appointments for sales team
- Consistently exceeded target calls by 15%
- Consistently exceeded appointments target by 10%

2001 to 2003, D'Arblay Connaught: **Customer Service Advisor**
1999 to 2001, Terrence Farrow & Partners: **Clerical Assistant**

Education:

Auto Credit Europe Training Centre
  NVQ Telephone Selling level 1
  NVQ Telephone Selling level 2

1998 to 1999, Bistock Secretarial College
  RSA Stage I Keyboard Skills
  RSA Stage I Office Skills

1991 to 1998, South West District School
  Five GCSEs, including Maths, English and French
  Two A levels – French and English

Personal details:

Date of birth: 3 May 1980

Health: Non-smoker

Interests: Team sports – netball, Women's League American football, volleyball

Full, clean UK driving licence

References available on request

Paul A Hendry
6 Yellow Stone Crescent
Headford
Staffordshire ST15 6YY

Tel: 0000 0000000

Career profile

An experienced store manager with a solid background in high-turnover supermarket environments in a wide variety of locations.

Key strengths

Experienced retail manager: 12 years' substantial experience gained with three high-turnover chains. Successful delivery of KPI and P&L strategies to achieve targets; full vocational training in all aspects of management from health and safety to EPOS.

Market knowledge: thorough understanding of local market requirements attested to by an increase in turnover of around £30,000 in total; constant review and analysis of local competitor activity and development of appropriate marketing strategy leading to sustained 10–15% annual growth.

Change manager: maintained level of turnover in Bath store despite extensive refurbishment by encouraging high level of commitment and focus in staff and making full use of available resources.

Career achievements

Starfrost Frozen Foods Ltd
2006 to present, various locations – four stores in all
Store Manager

- Increased turnover by around £10k in each of three different stores during time as manager
- Regularly achieved turnover of £25k–£40k, depending on store location
- Achieved a record-breaking Xmas turnover of £126k
- Maintained year-on-year increases of 10–15%
- Maintained level of turnover in Bath store despite extensive refurbishment
- Obtained wines and beers licence for two stores

- Improved stock control and shrinkage
- Supervised staff retraining

Freezer-Foods Ltd
1999 to 2006, various locations – 10 stores in all
Store Manager

- Increased turnover of Teddington store from £18k to £25k
- Increased turnover from £27k to £35k in Edgware store
- Increased annual turnover by an average of 15–20%
- Ensured each store was promoted to a higher division during time as manager
- Successfully handled two cases of gross misconduct
- Promoted from Assistant Manager in 2001

1998 to 1999
HMS Hollens
Manager
Bar manager on Royal Navy Base, responsible for the day-to-day running of the bar; organised staff, entertainment and administration.

Shield Market Ltd
1994 to 1998
Grocery Manager
Organised daily running of the department including hiring staff, ordering stock and achieving set targets. Promoted from Assistant Manager.

Hereford Stores Ltd
1990 to 1994
Assistant Grocery Manager
Organised daily running of grocery department including administration, staff training and customer service.

Various
1988 to 1990
Sales assistant and warehouse assistant – various positions.

Work-related training

Starfrost Frozen Foods Ltd:
    EPOS; FAST; OS2; STOP; SAS

Freezer-Foods Ltd Training Centre:
    Customer Care Awareness Course (Certificate)
    Basic Management Techniques
    Business Systems IBM Computer Course
    Instore Management EPOS Computer Course

ShieldCo Training Centre:
    Merchandising to Increase Sales
    Security Awareness
    Stock and Ordering
    Achieving Monthly Targets
    Health and Safety
    Staff Training, Appraisals and Motivation
    Staff Management Techniques

Personal details

Date of birth: 21 June 1972

Interests: Squash – local league player; cycling; skiing; water sports; foreign travel and cookery

Driving licence: Full, clean UK licence

Paige McLeod
Flat 2, 18 Brinsley Square
London SE17 7FS
Tel: 000 0000 0000
e-mail: pmcleod@anyisp.com

Career profile

Highly trained salesperson experienced in business-to-business sales and sales management, with a clear understanding of company structures and the decision-making process. A successful, profit-driven individual capable of making a significant contribution to the profitability of any employer.

Key strengths

Professional attitude: 15 years' sales experience with a clear track record of success leading to steady upward promotion. Member of the Professional Sales and Marketing Society and the Institute of Business, Sales and Marketing; diplomas in both Marketing and Management Studies and a certified diploma in Accounting and Finance.

Successful: a consistent track record of success including increasing sales by 15 per cent annually three years running in a heavily subscribed market; achieving a 120 per cent increase in uptake of technical support services, increasing both direct revenue and repeat orders from satisfied clients; winning Top Salesperson Award 2007; leading the highly successful team that won the top company award four times.

Key achievements

- *Mildenhall Business Systems:* Took region from fourth place to first place in two years by analysing sales statistics and seeing potential for growth, keeping a tight rein on stock and ordering levels; retraining staff in current sales practice.

- *The Business Business:* Expanded new territory and took it to second place nationally by setting team targets and ensuring they had the resources to meet them.

- *Direction Office Machines:* Established and developed virgin territory through extensive marketing campaign.

Career summary

Mildenhall Business Systems, 2006 to present
Regional Manager
Responsible for seven retail centres:

- Targeted technical support services and increased uptake by 120%
- Consistently exceeded targets
- Raised profile and increased enquiries by 25%
- Increased sales by 15%
- Improved profits by 12% overall
- Monitored sales statistics and controlled stock levels and ordering
- Assessed and trained sales staff

The Business Business, 2002 to 2006
Sales Manager
Responsible for own territory plus sales team of five people:

- Increased overall profits by 7–15%
- Consistently met and exceeded personal sales targets
- Set team sales budgets, assigned territories and targets
- Undertook staff reviews and training

Direction Office Machines, 1997 to 2002
Sales Executive

- Developed virgin territory
- Exceeded target performance by 5%
- Planned marketing campaigns for sales promotion
- Achieved 55% increase in enquiries at peak of promotion

Brook Copiers Ltd, 1995 to 1997
Sales Executive

- Exceeded all area sales targets
- Achieved Top Twenty National Sales Award

1992 to 1995, Various
Retail Sales, Telesales

Education and training

Member of the Professional Sales and Marketing Society

Institute of Business, Sales and Marketing
   2007 – Diploma in Management Studies
   2003 – Diploma in Marketing

Highbank College
   1996 – Certified Diploma in Accounting and Finance

Pinder Dobson School
   GCSEs: Five including Maths and English

Personal details

Date of birth:	17 October 1975
Health:	Non-smoker
Driving licence:	Full, clean UK licence
Interests:	Theatre and cinema
References:	Available on request

Francis Scott
12 Nuffield Crescent
Bowerby
Sunderland SN6 7ZP
Tel: 0000 0000000

Career profile:

A sales professional with solid experience in sales, marketing and management, and a history of success in both voluntary organisations and the private sector.

Key strengths:

Sales skills: a full range of skills developed over more than a decade in successful sales and marketing. Consistently achieved above-target sales and trained others in how to do so based on a customer-focused approach that attracted repeat orders from key customers on an ongoing basis.

Presentation skills: currently required to give effective yet enjoyable talks and presentations to the public, the media and other interested bodies to raise awareness of the Wellness Initiative and to secure donations. Donations last year totalled £3.5 million.

Leadership: a track record of over 10 years of motivating teams to set and achieve challenging targets and expect the very best from themselves. Feedback from teams demonstrates a confident, vigorous style of leadership based on sincere consultation allied with clear direction.

Key skills:

- Managing accounts and maintaining long-term customer relationships
- Motivating, developing and recruiting staff, including staff training and incentives
- Planning and controlling sales resources to maximum effect
- Maintaining cash flow and profitability
- Analysing and evaluating sales results
- Planning and implementing public relations and advertising campaigns

Career achievements:

2007 to present: The Wellness Initiative
Area Manager
Managed North East region of national medical charity:

- Worked towards Institute of Management NVQ level 4
- Took over and re-established area that had fallen into neglect
- Built up team of trained, professional volunteers
- Established efficient collection service
- Produced and implemented marketing plan
- Improved methods of forwarding donations

2004 to 2007: Dakk & Taylor Ltd
Sales/Product Manager

- Organised and established new product range from concept to completion
- Took over two neglected product ranges and revitalised them
- Organised continuous training programme for internal and external sales personnel with training in sales and product knowledge
- Planned and organised exhibitions and seminars
- Prepared and delivered presentations at all levels, including hands-on product demonstrations to groups of all sizes
- Directly responsible to the Managing Director and Sales and Marketing Director for all aspects relating to the promotion and sale of product range

1999 to 2004: Sensor (UK) Ltd
Product Manager

- Successfully increased sales year-on-year
- Maintained profitability of product range
- Organised consistently innovative public relations and advertising campaign
- Introduced and marketed new product ranges
- Trained and managed sales team
- Supervised customer orders and oversaw stock control

1995 to 1999: Avonside Ltd
Sales Manager

- Increased sales turnover
- Introduced new products and marketing ideas
- Recruited and trained sales team

1990 to 1995: FFG Co
Key Account Manager, Sales Representative
Proven ability as sales representative and promoted to Key Accounts
Manager in 1992.

Education:

Institute of Management
    NVQ Sales and Marketing Management level 4
Terrence Keeler Secondary School, 1978 to 1985
    A level: Mathematics
    GCSEs: seven including Maths and English

Personal details:

Date of birth: 11 March 1971

Health: Non-smoker

Interests: Badminton, riding, computing

Full, clean UK driving licence

References available on request

Ruth Sefton
78 Eastway Road
East Reach
Essex EX11 9AK
Tel: 0000 0000000
e-mail: rsefton@anyisp.com

Career profile

An innovative and intelligent media executive, with extensive experience of both planning and buying in all media.

Key strengths

Creativity: conceived, planned and implemented innovative media buying to remarkable effect for Callmate's 'Got you, babe' campaign, which increased their inquiry rate by 450 per cent and won an Ad-ept silver award.

Market analysis: in order to this achieve effective campaign, analysed target market and discovered lifestyle trend favouring use of low-cost early-morning cable TV slots, thereby obtaining maximum exposure to the target audience for a minimum budget.

Leadership: a consistent record of 'setting the pace' on projects and achieving goals through a balance of consultation and negotiation allied with vision and clear direction, an approach that I am told was instrumental in my achieving promotion within my current agency.

Career history

2008 – present: **The Advertising People**
Media Executive, Assistant Media Planner
Recommended appropriate and effective media for agency clients:

- Participated in preliminary talks with clients alongside Account Executive
- Analysed target market and marketing objectives
- Formulated media strategy
- Prepared detailed media plans
- Negotiated media rates
- Responsible for £2.5 million multimedia television account, and £1.75 million print media account

- Supervised current assistant planner
- Promoted from Assistant Media Planner to Media Executive in 2006

2005–2008: **Range, Klein and Morrisey**
Media Buyer

- Analysed data from NRS and BARB
- Prepared media strategy for direct-marketing clients
- Negotiated with media representatives for best rates
- Kept detailed records of all transactions

2002–2005: **The Word Factory**
Personal Assistant
Provided administrative support to Media Director and Media Department.

Education and training

North Western University
   BA English Literature (2.2)

Edward Marshall School
   GCSEs: seven including Maths and English
   A levels: English, French and History

Personal details

Date of birth:	21 June 1982
Interests:	Modern dance, fine art and antiques, travel
Driving licence:	Full, clean UK licence
References:	Available on request

Chapter Fourteen
CVs for technical jobs

The key thing the employer wants to know:
Can you do the job?

Technical personnel are required to carry out processes or production methods smoothly, accurately and efficiently.

It's important that a prospective employer reading your CV believes that you have the technical expertise – the knowledge and experience – to take over the vacancy efficiently, with as little disruption to the department as possible. In addition to answering the specific needs stated in the job ad, the most important areas to emphasise are your technical competence, experience, and qualifications and training, as these will be the best guide to your likely performance.

The key qualities employers usually look for in applicants for technical jobs are:

- specific technical skills;
- experience in particular areas;
- dependability and accuracy;
- a methodical approach;
- organisation;
- the ability to work with others.

What are the key points that differentiate a technical CV from those for other jobs?

Career profile

Use your Career profile to highlight the experience that brings competence and expertise, which are of value in many technical jobs.

Key qualifications

For many technical positions, your qualifications and training are the most important things you have to offer. However, if you simply move your Education and training section to the front page, you risk being mistaken for a college leaver without a Career history. The solution is to summarise your education and training in a Key qualifications section on the first page.

Qualifications and training relevant to the job you are applying for take priority. For example, you may be able to use several computer languages, but only the one or two used in *this* job need to go in the summary. The rest can be included in the Education and training section.

Key skills

As well as your Key qualifications, it's a good idea to include a non-academic Key skills section outlining your practical and/or managerial skills and experience.

Career history

Concentrate on the areas of responsibility you have covered, the skills you've used and the experience gained.

The examples on the following pages show CVs that make use of some or all of these points, and that include both a Key skills and a Key qualifications section.

The Technical CVs:

James Barossa – System controller.

Larraine Watt – Psychology research assistant.

Alison McInnery – Computer professional.

Robert Murray – Research Fellow.

John Crabb – Food technician.

This is the ad for a job James Barossa is applying for:

Data Services Manager

We are an international Customer Services Company and we seek a Data Services Manager to join our team to manage and deliver services to support the efficient and effective operation of the whole business.

You will need to have proven general administration skills and an excellent working knowledge of IT – especially Microsoft Office (including Access and Outlook) and systems management. The successful candidate will ideally be resourceful and ambitious, have good interpersonal skills and be a good communicator, be committed to the highest standards of quality, and be happy working both as part of a team and on their own initiative.

This role will possibly be ideal for a strong Administrator with an interest and key skills within IT. We will consider applicants from IT Support/ Technical backgrounds who are also able to demonstrate the key administrative skills required.

Apply to _____.

Turn to the next page to see how James used this job ad to give his CV added relevance by incorporating key information from it in his Career profile and Key strength sections.

JAMES BAROSSA
85 St Luke's Place
Collington
Berkshire BK6 2JZ
Tel: 0000 0000000
e-mail: jbarossa@anyisp.com

CAREER PROFILE

Versatile and proficient Data Services professional with an administration background and extensive IT support skills. Capable of making a significant contribution to the efficiency of any organisation.

KEY STRENGTHS

Proven administrative skills and an excellent working knowledge of IT: six years' experience providing full IT support to the South-East division (six offices, 200 staff) of a big insurance company, responsible for all administration associated with that role.

Resourceful, ambitious and committed: improved the efficiency of the system to the extent that claims once taking two weeks to process now take two days. Downtime for faults and malfunctions has decreased from 24 days a year to 3. Undertook HND in own time and expense to further my career and promoted to current position as a result.

Good interpersonal skills/good communicator: liaise between IT staff and the rest of the company at all levels; mentor and train new IT support staff and provide full information about the system status. I use a full range of interpersonal skills to achieve these tasks and also to evaluate user needs and assess problems in user-friendly, non-technical terms.

KEY SKILLS

- Ensuring the smooth running of all IT systems, including anti-virus software, print services and e-mail provision, providing users with appropriate support and advice and managing crises
- Supporting, facilitating and encouraging both effective usage and good practice
- Working in close cooperation with users and IT staff to clarify areas for change and development

- Evaluating user needs and system functionality and ensuring that IT facilities meet the needs of individuals and projects
- Planning, developing and implementing the IT budget, obtaining competitive prices from suppliers, where appropriate, to ensure cost-effectiveness
- Researching and installing new systems and scheduling upgrades
- Ensuring data security

KEY QUALIFICATIONS

City & Guilds Diploma in Computer Applications
PC Operating Systems – DOS and Windows, Unix, Word, Excel, Access, Outlook

CAREER SUMMARY

Perry & Wybrowe Insurance Ltd
2005 to present
System Controller
Supported 200 staff on six sites throughout the South of England using computerised systems:

- Provided help desk for software and hardware queries
- Used VMS and RSX Operating Systems to recover lost data files
- Analysed system performance, identified problems and established probable origin before taking appropriate action
- Logged errors for both software and hardware, and referred on to either programmers or engineer as appropriate
- Installed and implemented communications equipment using X21, Kilostream and Mercury links
- Backed up data records and transferred to off-site storage
- Maintained hardware and data wiring
- Promoted from Claims Supervisor to System Controller after completing City & Guilds training in 2001, in time to oversee computerisation of organisation

Ambassadors Assurance
2000 to 2005
Assistant Claims Supervisor, Clerk

EDUCATION AND TRAINING

Central Berkshire CAT
  2005 – City & Guilds Diploma in Computer Applications
The Willis School
  GCSEs: five including Maths and English

PERSONAL DETAILS

Date of birth:	2 January 1985
Health:	Non-smoker
Driving licence:	Full, clean UK licence
Interests:	Collecting early silent films and cine films, member of the English Film Archive
References:	Available on request

Larraine Watt
Flat 3, 14 Deans Gate Road
Waterly
Hertfordshire HE14 3GN

Tel. 0000 0000000
e-mail: lwatt@ncl.ac.uk

Career profile

Psychology graduate with a specific interest in education and development, especially as applied to adult learning, and practical experience of eliciting, collecting and analysing psychological data.

Key strengths

Project design: have coordinated, planned and run all stages of experiments including initial design, collecting data using a range of techniques such as observation, interviews and questionnaires; analysing data; writing detailed, comprehensive research reports and presenting the results.

Communication skills: achieving the best data requires tactful and effective communication with participants, which I always strive for. Presentation of initial ideas requires clarity and confidence if they are to be adopted, while completed reports must present results clearly and intelligibly if they are to be of value.

Initiative and commitment: responsible for initiating and proposing research into effects of stress on learning and carrying through design and implementation of project. Required to prioritise workload and manage day-to-day administrative organisation efficiently, while research projects mean working both competently and resourcefully under pressure to meet defined requirements. I believe colleagues and co-workers would agree that I am always happy to 'go the extra mile' when necessary.

Key qualifications

MSc The Psychology of Learning
BSc Psychology
    Advanced statistical analysis
    Quantitative techniques in applied research
    Experimental psychology
    The psychology of education and development

Career history

North London College, Centre for Educational Research, 2009 – present
Research Assistant
Conducted research into effects of relaxation and/or stress in learning situations with adult learners:

- Planned and arranged experiments with aim of providing specific research data
- Took participants through experimental procedures
- Collected and collated results
- Analysed preliminary data by computer
- Prepared preliminary report on findings

University of East England, 2004–2009
Research Assistant
Completed BSc and continued to MSc as research assistant to Professor Henry Jenkins, investigating the role of colour in children's play and development.

Assisted as demonstrator for undergraduate zoology practicals.

Education and training

University of East England
MSc The Psychology of Learning
BSc Psychology (2.1)

Kings Mordent School
GCSEs: eight including Maths, English and Biology
A levels: Biology, Chemistry and Sociology

Personal details

Date of birth: 14 May 1986

Interests: Singing with local musical society, modern and classical music, yoga

Health: Non-smoker

Driving licence: Full, clean UK licence

References: Available on request

Alison McInnery
91 Southways Road
East Studley
Surrey SR14 4OC
Tel: 0000 0000000
e-mail: amci@anyisp.com

Career profile

An experienced computer professional with a background in software development for structural engineering research and systems management, now specifically interested in the area of water resources or environmental science, and keen to gain experience leading to membership of the Chartered Institute of Water and Environmental Management.

Key skills and qualifications

- MSc Water Environment
- BSc (Hons) Ocean Science
- Mapping environmental, specifically hydrological, information via ARC/INFO Geographical Information System
- Using ORACLE/SQL*Plus database technology
- Pro*Fortran programming and environmental modelling

Career history

NAAC
Institute of Hydrology, Pardham, 2009 – present
MSc Placement
Mapped river-flow data for 1985 drought in Western Europe for completion of MSc dissertation:

- Contributed to UNESCO regional hydrology research project
- Identified gaps in time-series data, providing a basis for future research
- Produced map sequences for Western Europe, aiding presentation of the progress of the drought

Northern Power and Electric
Halford Technology Centre, Nordham, 2002–2007
Second Engineer
Analyst programmer:

- Developed 3-D computer graphics for finite element structural analysis resulting in external sales in the UK and overseas as well as internal use
- Provided CAD system management and technical support for internal and external clients

East Midlands Power Generating Board
Research Division, Stourling, 1996–2002
Technical Officer
Analyst programmer:

- Developed 3-D CAD graphics on IBM mainframe system
- Analysed data from computerised test rig
- Gave technical support on graphics hardware for engineering research throughout UK on network
- Promoted from laboratory technician in 1999

General employment
1991–1996
Computer operator
Mechanical engineer
ONC mechanical engineering apprentice

Education and training

2009 – present Downland University
MSc Water Environment
- Environmental Information Systems
- Water industry public relations and marketing
- Environmental law
- Project planning
- Operations and finance
- Ecological and adaptive management

2006–2009 University of the South West
BSc (Hons) Ocean Science
- Environmental modelling
- Sedimentation
- Underwater science
- Marine law and resources
- Physical oceanography

2001–2006 Open University
BA Science and Technology
- Computer-aided design
- Geology
- Imaging systems
- Information technology
- Oceanography

Computer skills
- DEC/VAX and SuperProject system management
- ARC/INFO geographical information system
- Silicon Graphics GL, GraPHIGS and IBM GDDM computer graphics
- UNIX operating system
- FORTRAN and 'C' programming
- Word, Access and Excel

Personal details

Date of birth: 5 June 1974

Driving licence: Full, clean UK licence

Interests: Cross-country running, gliding, swimming, sailing

References: Available on request

Robert Murray
12 Henshaw Place
Upper Tithing
Northamptonshire NP12 3GV
Tel: 0000 0000000
e-mail: rmurray@anyisp.com

Personal profile

A realistic, reliable and open-minded researcher with mathematical, statistical and organisational skills and broad experience in social research. A good team worker with a healthy sense of humour who works well under pressure.

Key strengths

Supervisory skills: supervised junior staff during course of research project, training them in the required techniques and monitoring performance, and have also managed staff in a retail environment.

Communication skills: working with interviewees on a sensitive subject required patience, tact and diplomacy. Clear and logical report-writing skills and good presentation skills required to present research findings effectively to both a medical and a non-medical audience.

Key skills

- Delivering all stages of a research project
  - writing proposals
  - questionnaire design
  - interviewing
  - data analysis
  - report writing and presentation
- Supervising junior staff
- Working with interviewees, requiring patience and diplomacy
- Computer-literate – Statistical Package for Social Sciences

Key qualifications

- BA (Hons) Applied Social Studies
- Diploma of the Market Research Society
- Use of Statistics in Medical Sociology
- Quantitative Techniques in Social Research

Career history

2007 – present
Northern and Western Medical School, Centre for Research on Drugs and
Health Behaviour
Research Fellow, Research Assistant
Conducted research into high-risk (HIV) behaviour of illicit drug users:

- Prepared and designed research project
- Supervised staff
- Interviewed high-risk groups
- Analysed resulting data
- Presented results

The results of this research project and subsequent publication and
presentation at a conference:

- validated the use of needle-exchange schemes
- helped attract further funding via other research programmes
- promoted extension of the scheme with a subsequent increase in
  staff levels

Rollandson Bookmakers, Tribune Bookmakers
1998–2002 Part-time, 1993–1998 Full-time
Manager
Responsible for all aspects of running a betting shop:

- Cash control
- Security
- Managing staff
- Accounts reconciliation
- Dealing appropriately with customers and clients

Education and training

2002–2006 City University
BA (Hons) Applied Social Studies 2:1
   Sociology
   Research methodology
   Computing
   Social policy
   Statistics
1990–1997 Oxhill Grammar School and College of Further Education
   GCSEs: seven including Maths and English
   A levels: English, French, History

Work-related training

Use of Statistics in Medical Sociology:
   applying statistical tests to quantitative data

Quantitative Techniques in Social Research:
   the application of quantitative techniques

Personal details

Date of birth:	7 November 1979
Driving licence:	Full, clean UK licence
Interests:	Most sports, including football, tennis, golf and snooker
References:	Available on request

John Crabb
1 Ascot Lane
Hills Barton
Cheshire CX14 8JN
Tel: 0000 0000000

Career profile

A food technician and supervisor with experience gained in all departments of food manufacturing, from Quality Control to New Product Development, together with a sound understanding of Total Quality Management.

Key strengths

Experience of automated procedures: I currently work for a large, automated producer in a supervisory role, responsible for the continued smooth running of the process and am consequently knowledgeable about all stages of production.

Appropriately qualified: HND in Food Technology from Southlands University; 12 years' experience in food production.

Supervisory skills: currently working as Department Supervisor with overall responsibility for all stages of manufacture and management of eight staff. Reduced downtime in the past year by 7 per cent through staff training and maintenance initiatives.

Key skills and qualifications

- BTEC HND Food Technology
- Extensive knowledge of the food manufacturing industry
- Managing and supervising staff
- Planning and executing product trials to budget
- Implementing laboratory requirements and techniques
- Understanding the importance of marketability and profitability

Professional experience

2007 to present
Cantrip Farms (Production) Ltd, Barton Magna
Department Supervisor
Worked in supervisory role in all areas of yogurt manufacturing from raw material to production through to cold store distribution:

- Improved process within natural-set department
- Reduced wastage in custard-style yogurt department
- Improved efficiency overall, reducing costs and improving profit margins

2005 to 2007
Hilldean Dairies Ltd, Pollend
New Product Development Technician
Developed marketing ideas into manufacturable products:

- Developed key product ranges, improving market placement
- Increased product diversity and, consequently, viability within group
- Consistently brought processing trials in to time and on budget

2001 to 2005
Farm Fresh Foods Ltd, Millingham
Senior Laboratory Assistant
Responsible for quality control of all incoming raw materials and supervision of staff in the absence of the Quality Control Supervisor. Promoted from Laboratory Assistant in 2003.

Education and training

1998 to 2001, Southlands University, Sunderford
BTEC HND Food Technology

1996 to 1998, Pentland College of Agriculture and Horticulture, Pentland
BTEC OND Food Technology

1991 to 1996, Bower Park School, Alston
Total of five GCSEs gained, including Maths and English

Personal

Date of birth: 10 May 1980

Driving licence: Full, clean UK licence

Health: Non-smoker

Interests: I have a keen interest in sport and keeping fit, and play regularly for a local Sunday football team.

References: Available on request

Chapter Fifteen
CVs for management jobs

The key thing the employer wants to know:
Will you get results?

Managers ensure that things happen as and when they should within an organisation so that targets are met and results are achieved. It's a manager's job to see that their personnel can carry out their own jobs effectively and efficiently.

It's essential a prospective employer believes that you will be an effective manager. As well as focusing on the employer's needs as stated in the job ad, it's also important to emphasise your past achievements in your CV, as these will be a good indication of your future abilities.

The key qualities employers usually look for in applicants for management jobs are:

- the ability to get results;
- the ability to motivate and manage others;
- competence, reliability and responsibility;
- tenacity and perseverance, along with energy, commitment and enthusiasm;
- the ability to tackle problems effectively.

What will help get these qualities across?

Career profile

Personal qualities often count in management positions. Include these in a Career profile to highlight your special characteristics. Outline your own personal style of management and the experience you've had to develop and exercise these qualities.

Key achievements

Companies want managers who can make a difference to performance – achievements matter. Include a Key achievements section, either with or instead of a Key skills section. Let them know what you're capable of doing.

Career history

Put facts and figures to the claims you have made. Rather than just stating your responsibilities, give details of your performance with past companies and expand on your achievements and results. Your experience of encountering and solving problems is important as well.

The examples on the following pages show CVs that make use of some or all of the above points, including a Key achievements section. The Management CVs:

Aldwin Hills – Financial manager.

Linda Vernon – Catering manager.

Mark Renato – Operations manager.

Ellen Ashe – Personnel manager.

Lee Daniels – Technical manager.

This is the job ad that attracted Aldwin Hills attention:

Business Development Consultant

Are you someone special?

This is a fantastic opportunity to join one of the leaders in providing management solutions. We are known for bringing a variety of skills and experience to meet challenging client requirements and we need a Business Development Consultant to join our team.

You will be pragmatic with a wealth of experience at senior executive level and a bias towards practical solutions with the ability to relate to the needs of a range of businesses.

You may have run your own successful business, held a training role in a corporate or finance business, or have a proven track record in profit responsibility for a medium/large organisation.

You will have excellent communication and interpersonal skills and an outstanding degree of business acumen.

If this sounds like you, send your CV to _____.

The next page shows how Aldwin made use of the information in this ad to customise his CV so that it clearly demonstrated his suitability for the job.

Aldwin Hills
7 White Hart Villas
Wood Heath
Norfolk NF11 6DM
Tel: 0000 0000000

Career profile:

LAUTRO-trained financial consultant with a wealth of experience dealing with corporate solutions, a proven talent for business planning and forecasting, and a management background gained in both manufacturing and services.

Key strengths:

A wealth of experience at senior executive level: Eight years' experience at senior management level, including marketing, finance and project management with large and medium-sized organisations.

Outstanding degree of business acumen: Currently running own successful management consultancy advising on budgeting, planning and forecasting in order to improve accuracy, timeliness and efficiency with up to 25 per cent performance increases.

Ability to relate to the needs of a range of businesses: Have provided financial advice, marketing management and project management for a range of organisations, from a venture capital company to haulage companies and wholesalers.

Key achievements:

- Improving performance of client organisations by 5–25% overall, including:
  - ABC UK Ltd
  - Xpress Haulage
  - Cornwallis Systems Ltd
- Establishing a venture capital company in the UK on behalf of the parent company
- Bringing the project in on budget and generating £4 million of business in the first three months

Career history:

2006 – ongoing
Management Consultant

- Analysed and advised on aspects of business finance:
  - Analysing financial data and monitoring financial control
  - Producing budgets, cash-flow forecasts, and profit and loss projections
  - Analysing and processing productivity records
  - Assisting businesses to develop in a realistic and viable way
- Advised companies wanting to raise finance
- Compiled guidelines and yardsticks for companies wishing to monitor their performance and develop further, including: Market segmentation; Financial controls; Production; Product/service development
- Prepared and presented business plans, including break-even analysis

Maynard Investment Corporation (Portland International)
2004–2006
Project Manager
Established UK subsidiary for overseas investment corporation:

- Researched and analysed market
- Created venture capital company and established company's presence in the UK
- Installed and implemented all administrative systems
- Administered all documentation, agreements and financial analyses
- Achieved early break-even by keeping well within budget
- Generated over £4 million of business within three months of UK launch

Preston and Fielding
2002–2004
Financial Adviser
Analysed clients' current situations and future goals. Advised and assisted them to plan and monitor their financial situation. Trained and qualified by LAUTRO.

Hoopers Ltd
1998–2002
Sales and Marketing Executive
Sold, marketed and promoted garden products to single and multiple garden centres and similar outlets.

Willings & Cathar Wholesale Blinds Ltd
1983–1998
Sales Director
Started as general assistant and reached director level with responsibility
for group.

Work-related training:

Computer skills:
    CLAIT
    List Manager – Xerox Corporation course on building and maintaining
       databases
    Microsoft Office: Word, Excel, Access, PowerPoint
Other:
    Business Planning and Good Business Practice
    Taxation, Annual Accounts and HMRC
    Advertising and Promotion
    Marketing – Planning and Implementation
    Direct Marketing
    Negotiating Skills
    Customer Care

Personal details:

Date of birth: 16 September 1967

Interests: Member of the Wood Heath Photographic Society and
the Enterprise Business Club, active in the PDSA and
the North Norfolk Performing Arts Committee. Enjoy
swimming and walking

Car owner/driver with full, clean UK licence

References available on request

Linda Vernon
33 Shortmead Road
Allerton
Derbyshire DB3 5TF

Tel: 0000 0000000

Personal profile

Confident and creative manager with significant experience in both catering and management gained with major employers in the field, and proven skills in setting and achieving goals through the development and motivation of staff.

Key strengths

Restaurant management experience: two years as assistant manager of La Noisette Restaurant with full responsibility for daily functions.

Drive and motivation: promoted steadily from Catering Assistant to Assistant Manager of a leading restaurant, I have never held a job without improving efficiency or bringing in new business. Personally undertook extensive staff retraining programme at La Noisette to make service something truly memorable.

Key skills and achievements

- Six years' experience in restaurant and catering management
- Improving efficiency of service in two significantly different environments
- Successfully introducing comprehensive staff training programmes
- Establishing systems and procedures for a large-scale catering operation
- Managing a first-class restaurant

Career history

2009 to present
La Noisette Restaurant
Assistant Manager
Responsible for day-to-day running of restaurant and management of 10 restaurant-area and bar staff. Duties included:

- budgeting
- stock control
- ordering
- bookings
- customer service

Introduced comprehensive staff training schedules, resulting in a greatly improved service to customers and the continued enhancement of La Noisette's first-class reputation.

2006 to 2009
Lambourne Health Trust
Catering Supply Manager
Full responsibility for planning and delivery of catering service to two hospitals, four nursing homes and four residential facilities. Duties included:

- full budget planning
- service administration
- management of up to 20 staff

Improvement of service efficiency resulted in reduction of service costs by 12%.

2004 to 2006
Hollander Catering
Assistant Manager
Responsible for day-to-day organisation of a commercial catering company including both office and staff administration.
    Planned and delivered presentations for company which won two major new contracts.

2002 to 2004
Cornfleet Country Club
Food Store and Cellar Manager/Banqueting Assistant
Responsible for supervision of all stock ordering and deliveries for cellars and food stores, and organisation of table layouts for all function rooms.

2000 to 2002
Various
Waitress/Catering Assistant
General waitress duties including providing breakfast, lunch and dinner to 550 people daily, and silver service in a five-star country hotel.

Education and training

Professional training:
Restaurant and Catering Training Association
NVQ level 3 Catering
NVQ level 3 Catering Management
NVQ level 4 Business Management

Dorning College of Technology, Combe, Dorset, 1998 to 2000
City & Guilds Catering Certificate

Bordingham Comprehensive, Bordingham, Dorset, 1993 to 1998
Total of seven GCSEs, including Maths and English

Personal details

Date of birth:	12 April 1982
Driving licence:	Full, clean UK licence
	Hygiene Certificates held
	St John's Ambulance First Aid certificate held
Interests:	Active member of local environmental group, member of the Wine Society
References:	Available on request

Mark Renato
43 Redding Pit Road
Heath Place
West Sussex SX15 8DD
Tel: 0000 0000000
e-mail: mrenato@bishopgroup.co.uk

Career profile:

An Operations Manager with a total of 15 years' manufacturing experience including seven years at senior management level. An effective communicator and motivator with a track record of achievement in implementing change successfully and efficiently, based on a thorough understanding of engineering processes.

Key strengths:

Solution-focused: devised and implemented development plan for two subsidiary factories, increasing efficiency by 12 per cent, which put them on an equal footing with the rest of the company.

Understanding of employee relations and excellent communication skills: required to negotiate effectively with clients and suppliers, including the MOD and Crown Suppliers, as well as other members of staff. Improved long-standing difficulties in industrial relations at acquired site and restored management leadership with a package of measures including a negotiated Partnership Agreement, which increased productivity by 15 per cent.

Self-motivated: committed to a programme of continued vocational training including negotiating skills, office-appropriate IT skills, and management skills.

Key achievements:

- Increasing financial performance of group by £250k overall
- Reducing duplicated operating costs by £100k per annum
- Managing and coordinating activities at three factory sites and ensuring efficient supply of products to customers
- Reorganising and establishing Administrative Support Centre
- Drawing up and implementing change programme in two subsidiary factories, bringing them level with rest of group
- Improving industrial relations, restoring management leadership with help of Partnership Agreement

Career history:

2008 to present
Bishop & Challenger Ltd
Operations Manager
Responsible for factories and staff within the operational area:

- Coordinated and managed activities within three factories and an Administrative Centre
- Organised efficient running of sites
- Ensured delivery of products to internal and external customers
- Managed quality control, budget and timetable requirements
- Prepared budgets and allocated capital expenditure

2005 to 2008
Deans Valley Forgeway Ltd
Factory Manager
Responsible for all aspects of factory management:

- Achieved budget production levels
- Administered Health and Safety legislation
- Prepared budgets
- Allocated capital expenditure
- Liaised with customers, notably MOD and Crown Suppliers

Esbarten Engineering Ltd
2001 to 2005
Industrial Engineer
Responsible for engineering services at factory and regional level. Provided production engineering service with particular emphasis on product costing, pre-production engineering and methods assessment and improvement.

1997 to 2001
Peckham & Been Associates Ltd
Design and Development Engineer
Designed and developed prototypes from inception through to production. Promoted from apprentice level in 1999.

Work-related training:

Computer skills:
    CLAIT
    Computer Smartware II
    Microsoft Office: Word, Excel, Access
Other:
    Open University – The Effective Manager
    City & Guilds – Certificate in Mechanical Engineering
    Supplementary Certificates in:
        Toolroom Practices
        Inspection and Quality Assurance
        Health and Safety Legislation
        Negotiating Skills

Personal details:

Date of birth: 1 October 1982

Interests: Swimming, golf, member of West Sussex Choral Society, voluntary trainer with the Southey Youth Association

Car owner/driver with full, clean UK licence

References available on request

Ellen Ashe
91 Stuart Close, Reach
Gloucester GL4 7XS
Tel: home: 0000 000000, mobile: 0000 000000

CAREER PROFILE

Experienced personnel manager with expertise in both human resources and industrial relations, and with general management skills including administration and project leadership as well as overall staff management.

KEY STRENGTHS

Knowledge of psychometric testing: qualified in the use of psychometric and profiling tools and have since administered over 250 tests, leading to better staff functioning and a noticeable increase in retention.

Professional attitude: Fellow of the Institute of Personnel and Development; 12 years' experience in HR, promoted three times within the same company; continuing programme of self-development through specialist vocational training.

Executive-level recruitment: organised complete personnel function for Cotswolds Head Office; successfully recruited Financial Director and Assistant Director as well as other key management personnel.

KEY ACHIEVEMENTS

- Developing comprehensive human resource policy, reducing staff turnover and increasing efficiency and productivity
- Negotiating Partnership Agreement between management and unions
- Achieving 85% staff compliance with 24-hour telephone banking service
- Introducing Quality Programme of personnel-led productivity initiatives
- Devising and delivering focused induction training course to 350 employees
- Fellow of the Institute of Personnel and Development
- Qualified in the use of psychometric testing and profiling tools

CAREER HISTORY

2005 to present
Cotswolds Financial Services Group, Employee Relations Manager
Managed overall personnel function for office and general staff:

- Undertook
  - complete IR function
  - specialist employment consultancy
  - project management
  - social club management
- Developed personnel policies and procedures for financial group
- Improved effectiveness of human resource development strategies
- Managed introduction of performance evaluation system
- Extended skills in all aspects of personnel management
- Developed comprehensive knowledge of employment law, performance management and discipline handling

1996 to 2005
Personnel Manager (Sales Staff), Personnel Manager (Head Office Staff)
Organised complete personnel function for Head Office and Southern Region Staff:

- Managed personnel function for field-based staff, locally based office and general staff
- Administered records, pay and contractual documents
- Promoted from assistant personnel officer in 1990

1992 to 1996
Personnel Administration Supervisor
Responsible for administration of:

- records
- information
- pay
- contractual documents

1988 to 1992
Personnel Assistant
Administrative and semi-technical support.

1982 to 1988
Clerical Assistant and Officer

- Personnel administration including recruitment, salaries, expenses, cash accounting
- Routine tax returns and administrative duties

EDUCATION AND TRAINING

Work-related training:

- Psychometric testing
- Assessment skills
- Management training courses

Other:
Fardean College, 1986 to 1988
A levels: British Government, Economics
Episcopal Secondary School, 1976 to 1982
GCSEs: Six including Maths, Economics and English

Professional:
Fellow of the Institute of Personnel and Development

PERSONAL

Date of birth:	17 October 1965
Health:	Non-smoker
Driving licence:	Full, clean UK licence
Interests:	Table tennis, including running local club; photography, City & Guilds qualified; swimming; music; voluntary work

Lee Daniels
42 Cartwright Crescent
St George
Bedford BD12 7GM

Tel: Home: 0000 0000000, Work: 0000 0000000
e-mail: ldaniels@easternaero.co.uk

CAREER PROFILE

A challenging senior management position with a progressive company sought by an experienced Engineering Production Manager with 10 years' management experience, a strong background in aeronautical engineering and a high degree of technical as well as managerial skill.

KEY STRENGTHS

Change manager with strong leadership skills: successfully administered closure of Eastern Aero-Engines London repair facility and transfer to Dublin with minimum disruption – plant fully operational within two weeks. Devised, negotiated and introduced new working practices to facilitate a steady 7–10 per cent annual growth in a more commercial environment.

Understanding of the aeronautical industry: extensive knowledge and experience gleaned during a career in the industry, from project management and systems design through to production management. Member of the team responsible for bringing the B77 engine from development into production.

KEY SKILLS

- Professional management skills:
    - meeting objectives
    - identifying problems
    - promoting solutions
    - managing change
    - setting and monitoring policy
    - motivating and developing staff
- Extensive experience of aero-engine overhaul and repair management
- Knowledge of business systems with contracts experience
- Well-developed and effective communication skills

CAREER HISTORY

2008 – present
Eastern Aero-Engines plc
Engine Overhaul Manager
Responsible for developing a sustainable and profitable Sea-horse repair business on engines, components and associated services:

- Achieved planned margins and cash flow
- Developed market opportunities and expanded business
- Negotiated contracts
- Interfaced with customers
- Allocated and managed resources to fulfil target commitments

Also administered closure of East London Repair Facility and transfer to Dublin.

2001–2008
Repair Control Manager
Responsible for administration during contractual changes from Cost Plus to Fixed Price:

- Introduced new working practices to suit commercial environment
- Supervised contract administration
- Coordinated technical control and facility planning
- Maintained customer interface

Engines worked: Sea-horse, SD222 and Blair conversions.

1999–2001
Production Control Manager
Responsible for scheduling and logistic support of engine/module build programmes. Developed mechanical scheduling/monitoring and reporting system.

1995–1999
Inventory Manager
Responsible for order administration and inventory management for new engine projects. Planned and commissioned new Finished Parts Store (£1 million project).

1988–1995
Systems Designer
Responsible for SDA system. Trialled SDA packages. Designed order entry systems.

1986–1988
Project Manager
Responsible for bringing B77 engine from development into production.

1983–1986
Section Leader

QUALIFICATIONS

MIEE
HND Production Engineering
A levels: Maths, Physics

Work-related training:
    Financial Management
    Appraisal Techniques
    Quality Control

PERSONAL DETAILS

Date of birth:	1 June 1964
Driving licence:	Full, clean UK licence
Interests:	Sailing, hill-walking
References:	Available on request

Chapter Sixteen
Never be lost for words

Finding the right word is often one of the hardest parts of writing a CV. This chapter has examples of positive words and phrases for you to use, which might help you to expand those vital keywords, and also remind you of skills and qualities you want to include. It contains:

- positive characteristics;
- action words;
- positive descriptions;
- benefits;
- desirable qualities.

Positive characteristics

These words describe personal attributes that are often seen as positive and useful in the workplace. Choose the words that describe you best:

Able	Accurate	Adaptable
Adroit	Adventurous	Alert
Ambitious	Analytical	Appreciative
Articulate	Assertive	Astute
Attractive	Bilingual	Bright
Calm	Capable	Competent

Confident	Consistent	Cooperative
Creative	Decisive	Dedicated
Dependable	Diligent	Diplomatic
Dynamic	Educated	Effective
Efficient	Energetic	Enthusiastic
Experienced	Expert	Fast
Firm	Fit	Flexible
Friendly	Gregarious	Hardworking
Healthy	Honest	Human
Humane	Imaginative	Independent
Informed	Ingenious	Innovative
Intelligent	Inventive	Knowledgeable
Literate	Loyal	Mature
Methodical	Motivated	Multilingual
Non-smoking	Objective	Open-minded
Organised	Outgoing	Outstanding
Patient	People-oriented	Perceptive
Persistent	Personable	Pioneering
Poised	Practical	Principled
Productive	Professional	Proficient
Punctual	Qualified	Quick
Quick-thinking	Rational	Ready
Realistic	Reliable	Resourceful
Responsible	Robust	Scrupulous
Self-assured	Self-confident	Self-motivated
Self-reliant	Sensitive	Serious
Shrewd	Skilled	Smart
Spirited	Stable	Strong
Successful	Supportive	Tactful
Talented	Tenacious	Thorough
Thoughtful	Trained	Trustworthy

Versatile	Vigorous	Well-educated
Well-groomed	Willing	Witty
Young		Youthful

Action words

These are positive, active words that you can use to describe your responsibilities and achievements.

(All the words here are in the past tense – they all end in 'ed' – which is right for the Career history section of your CV. If you want to use them in the Key skills section, change the 'ed' to 'ing' to turn it into the present tense; for example:

Key skills: Organising meetings and functions, purchasing stationery

Career history: Organised meetings and functions, purchased stationery)

Accelerated	Accessed	Achieved
Acquired	Acted	Administered
Advised	Analysed	Appointed
Appraised	Arranged	Assigned
Assisted	Attended	Booked
Broadened	Budgeted	Checked
Coached	Collaborated	Competed
Completed	Communicated	Compiled
Conceived	Conducted	Consulted
Contributed	Controlled	Coordinated
Correlated	Created	Delegated
Demonstrated	Designed	Determined
Developed	Devised	Diagnosed
Directed	Doubled	Edited
Effected	Eliminated	Enabled

Established	Evaluated	Executed
Exercised	Expanded	Expedited
Explored	Facilitated	Fostered
Formulated	Founded	Generated
Guided	Handled	Harmonised
Headed	Helped	Hired
Identified	Implemented	Improved
Increased	Initiated	Installed
Instituted	Instructed	Interacted
Invented	Investigated	Launched
Led	Liaised	Maintained
Managed	Marketed	Mentored
Monitored	Motivated	Negotiated
Opened	Operated	Organised
Oversaw	Participated	Performed
Pinpointed	Pioneered	Planned
Prepared	Presented	Processed
Produced	Programmed	Promoted
Proposed	Provided	Purchased
Recommended	Recruited	Recorded
Reduced	Reorganised	Reported
Represented	Researched	Resolved
Restored	Restructured	Reviewed
Revised	Saved	Scheduled
Secured	Selected	Set up
Shaped	Sold	Solved
Structured	Supervised	Taught
Tested	Trained	Upgraded
Used	Utilised	Visualised
Won	Wrote	

Positive descriptions

As well as using positive words for your characteristics and achievements, there is also a variety of ways to describe your strengths.

Instead of saying 'I am good at ...', you could say:

I am skilled at ...	I am a skilful ...
I possess a degree of ability in ...	I am very good at ...
I am extremely good at ...	I have exceptional ...
I am adept at ...	I am an expert in ...
I excel at ...	I have the ability to ...
I am competent in ...	I am an experienced ...
I am a deft ...	I have a talent for ...
I am familiar with ...	I am qualified to ...

For example:

I am skilled at facilitating the exchange of ideas.

I have exceptional communication skills.

I have a high degree of ability in computer programming.

I am adept at promoting policy changes.

I am very good at handling a variety of tasks efficiently.

I am exceptional at motivating large or small groups.

I have a talent for budget projection.

I am familiar with a wide range of software.

I am qualified to assess retail training up to NVQ level 3.

Benefits

Employers want to feel confident that the person they employ will take problems off their hands. They are looking for people who can do any of the following:

Increase	Decrease	Improve
Profits	Staff turnover	Competitive advantage
Product turnover	Risks	
Sales	Time taken	Appearance and/or marketability
Efficiency	Potential problems	
Market opportunities	Costs	Organisation
	Waste	Information flow
		Staff performance
		Teamwork and relationships

Make sure your CV includes any of the above benefits that you have achieved in your job.

Desirable qualities

The following characteristics are rated the most desirable by the majority of employers. Although many of them seem quite obvious, they are the sort of things that can easily be forgotten when thinking about your qualities and characteristics. Keep them in mind when writing your CV and include them, where relevant and appropriate, in your personal profile or career profile.

Employers prefer someone who is:

reliable;

punctual;

trustworthy;

friendly;

willing to learn;

enthusiastic;

accurate;

able to work as part of a team;

able to follow instructions accurately;

able to handle problems, and refer them on, appropriately;

able to work with colleagues, customers or clients.

Employers look for someone who:

has a positive attitude;

takes pride in their work;

has a professional appearance;

has initiative.

Putting it together

Use the template CV on the next page as a guide to where you might find suitable words and phrases for each particular section.

Play around with the words in this chapter and the examples in Chapter 2 until you arrive at something that describes both you and the work you have done, accurately and positively.

Don't forget to mine the job ad or job description for ideas. Read several ads for the sort of job you intend to apply for to give you a feel for the sort of descriptive words that are used in your particular field. You can include those that apply to you in your CV. See Chapters 2 and 3 for more on this topic, and look at Chapter 5 for advice about keywords.

NAME
Address
Contact details

Career profile

(Look at **Positive characteristics**, **Positive descriptions** and **Desirable qualities**)

_____

_____

_____

_____

Key strengths

(Look at **Positive descriptions**, **Benefits**, **Desirable qualities** and **Action words**)

_____

_____

_____

Key skills

(Look at **Positive descriptions** and **Action words**)

_____

_____

_____

_____

Career history

(Name of company)
(Dates you worked there)
(Job title)
(Job responsibilities. Look at **Action words**)

_____

_____

_____

(Achievements and responsibilities. Look at **Action words** and **Benefits**)

_____

_____

_____

(Name of company)
(Dates you worked there)
(Job title)
(Job responsibilities. Look at **Action words**)

_____

_____

_____

(Achievements and responsibilities. Look at **Action words** and **Benefits**)

_____

_____

_____